What
WE HOPE
For

Mastering the Life-Changing Skills
That Are the Pillars of Hope

DUSTIN DRAKE, PH.D.

To reach out to the author or publisher, contact via email at info@whatwehopefor.com.

Additional information and resources can be found at whatWEHOPEfor.com along with supplemental guidebooks and offers.

This book contains advice and information relating to health care. It should be used to supplement rather than replace the advice of your doctor or another trained health professional. If you know or suspect that you have a health problem, it is recommended that you seek the advice of a competent professional before embarking on any medical program or treatment. All efforts have been made to assure the accuracy of the information contained in this book as of the date of publication. This publisher and the author disclaim liability for any medical outcomes that may occur as a result of applying the methods suggested in this book.

ISBN: 979-8-9994553-1-4 (ebook)
ISBN: 979-8-9994553-0-7 (paperback)
ISBN: 979-8-9994553-2-1 (hardback)
ISBN: 979-8-9994553-3-8 (audiobook)
Library of Congress Control Number: 2025918399

First edition 2025

To my wife and kids.
You are and always will be the entirety of
my hopes and dreams.

Table of Contents

Part 1: A Foundation of Hope

Part 2: The Six Pillars of Hope

Part 3: Beyond The Pinnacle

Acknowledgements

This book could not have been completed without the help and support of a number of people. There are too many of you to thank individually, so know that you are appreciated.

James Sparks is a co-creator of the WE HOPE framework, and he is main contributor to the content of this book. Thank you for being a great partner in the development of these concepts and for helping live my purpose.

To my wife and kids, thanks for always helping me find ways to be better. I am honestly one of the most fortunate men on earth because of you. You are my hope!

To the main individuals who helped review this book prior to publishing, I appreciate your contributions and your insights. I will be forever grateful for your willingness to jump at the opportunity to criticize me, and I am better for it.

Last, I would like the readers to know that the content of this book has been developed over the last 10 years. I have used AI as an editing tool, but all structure and concepts were researched, written, and organized by James and myself well before AI existed. I have also completed multiple final edits and rewrites to ensure that my message lives up to my expectations.

A Note from the Author

I've never been the best at anything. I'm not a bestselling author or a millionaire entrepreneur. I didn't break records as an athlete. I chose education as my profession when I could have sought wealth through a different career path.

I come from the kind of background that doesn't usually make book jackets: middle-class, middle-of-the-road, middle America.

I feel like that's also what makes this message matter.

I've built a life that works. It isn't flashy or viral, but it's real. I'm an educator, a partner, a dad. I've made peace with my gifts and my limitations and learned how to live with hope even when the big wins didn't come the way I thought they would.

My superpower, if I have one, is being **average** and finding meaning there.

This book isn't coming from someone who "made it big." It's coming from someone who's **made life big**, a sustainable, purposeful, impactful life. If that's what you're after, too, I believe this framework can help you find your way forward.

I honestly believe that the promise of the WE HOPE framework can lead you to the highest levels of personal and professional success if that's what you really HOPE for. At the same time, the beauty of the framework is found in living an ordinary life filled with extraordinary meaning, which is what all of us should really HOPE for.

Part 1

A Foundation of Hope

Introduction
What WE HOPE For

I didn't realize I was drowning until I was already underwater. For thirteen years, I had been called "Mr. Drake" or "Dr. Drake" or just "Drake" by my students. I was the teacher who showed up early, stayed late, and genuinely believed that education could change lives. I had built my identity around being the one who saw potential in every kid who walked through my door, especially the ones other teachers had written off.

Purpose is a funny thing. It can keep you running on empty longer than you should, long after you've lost joy, clarity, or even a sense of who you are outside your title. When the systems you're trying to fix keep breaking, when the outcomes don't match your effort, that sense of purpose starts to fade. It doesn't leave with fireworks or alarms. It erodes quietly, one unremarkable day at a time.

I remember the moment I knew something was deeply wrong. I was sitting at my desk after school, staring at the same pile of reports that needed my attention. I'd been trying to work on them for hours. I hadn't moved. I hadn't spoken. My office was silent, and I was numb. It was as if I had become background noise in my own life.

A colleague knocked on my door and asked if I was okay. I smiled automatically and said, "Yeah, just tired." Something in my voice betrayed me. I wasn't just tired. I was done.

What I was feeling wasn't just exhaustion but a quiet, persistent hopelessness that I didn't know how to name at the time. It wasn't dramatic. It wasn't a breakdown. It was just emptiness.

Before that, I used to be good at showing up. I don't mean just physically, though I did that too. I was the one who stayed after meetings to stack chairs, who volunteered for the thankless committee work, and who said yes when everyone else was suddenly busy. I built my identity around being reliable, the person others could count on when things got messy.

For years, that felt like enough, more than enough. It felt like purpose. Then something started to shift, gradually. I didn't notice it at first. Getting out of bed required a little more negotiation with myself each morning. Conversations I used to enjoy started feeling like performances I had to manage. The energy I'd always counted on began running lower, staying empty longer.

I told myself it was seasonal. It was just work stress or too much caffeine, not enough sleep. The usual suspects we blame when life starts feeling harder than it should.

Seasons changed, and the heaviness didn't lift. The disconnection crept in through the smallest cracks first. I'd find myself staring at my phone, scrolling through the same feeds without reading anything, killing time I didn't remember deciding to waste. Emails sat unanswered not because they were difficult, but because responding felt like lifting something impossibly heavy.

I wasn't falling apart in any dramatic way. I was still getting by, showing up to commitments, preparing lessons, and smiling at the right moments. Inside, though, I was starting to feel like I was watching my own life from a distance, present but not really there, going through motions that used to mean something.

The reliable person everyone knew me as was still functioning, but the person inside that reliable exterior was disappearing piece by piece. I'd catch myself mid-conversation, realizing I hadn't heard the last several sentences because my mind had drifted somewhere else entirely. Food lost its taste. Life became background noise. Even things I'd once been passionate about felt flat, like someone had drained all the color from a photograph.

Maybe you know this feeling. It doesn't feel like the kind of crisis that demands immediate attention, but the quieter kind that settles in like background noise. You're functioning, so it doesn't count as a breakdown. You're not in danger, so it doesn't warrant concern. You just feel less like yourself than you used to.

This disconnection touches everything. You lose touch with your purpose first, the sense that what you're doing matters in any meaningful way. The work that once energized you becomes a series of tasks to complete. The relationships that once sustained you become social obligations to manage. The future that once excited you becomes a vague concept you can't quite grasp.

Then comes the disconnection from your body. You forget to eat, or you eat without tasting. You sleep without resting. You move through space without inhabiting it. Your body becomes a vehicle you're operating rather than a home you're living in. Physical symptoms appear that doctors can't quite explain.[1] Headaches, digestive issues, mysterious aches can come and go without clear cause.

Joy becomes a memory rather than an experience. Things that used to bring you pleasure feel hollow. Celebrations feel like performances. Laughter feels forced. You find yourself going through the motions of happiness while feeling nothing at all. The absence isn't painful in an acute way. It's more like discovering you've been colorblind your whole life and only now noticing that everyone else sees something you can't.

Your sense of worth erodes so slowly you don't notice until it's nearly gone. The voice in your head that used to offer encouragement turns critical. The inner dialogue that once supported your decisions becomes a constant stream of second-guessing.

You start believing that maybe you were never as capable as you thought, never as valuable as others claimed, never as worthy of good things as you'd imagined.

People become distant even when they're sitting right next to you. Conversations feel scripted. Intimacy feels impossible. You find yourself performing the role of yourself in your own relationships, saying what you think you should say, showing up how you think you should show up, all while feeling completely alone inside your own life.

That's where I was when I realized I needed to understand what had happened to me, what had happened to my hope.

The truth is that you're not the only one experiencing this quiet crisis. We're living through what researchers are calling an epidemic of disconnection.[2] Mental health statistics tell part of the story, but they don't capture the millions of people who aren't clinically depressed or anxious but who are simply existing in the gray space between thriving and suffering.

Recent research reveals the scope of this crisis. The U.S. Surgeon General declared loneliness a public health epidemic, noting that about one in two adults in America reported experiencing loneliness.[3] The World Health Organization reports that around 16% of people worldwide—one in six—experience loneliness.[4] Perhaps most telling, a 2024 study found that 30% of American adults felt lonely at least weekly over the past year, while 10% reported feeling lonely every day.[5]

This isn't just about feeling sad or isolated. Research shows that 81% of adults who were lonely also suffered with anxiety or depression compared to 29% of those who were less lonely, revealing a complex interaction where loneliness, anxiety, and depression all feed into each other.[6] The implications extend far beyond emotional well-being, affecting physical health, cognitive function, and overall life satisfaction.

You don't have to work in education to know what these things feels like. Maybe for you it wasn't a school office. Maybe it was a corporate cubicle, a hospital corridor, a kitchen table covered in bills, or your own car parked outside your house because you couldn't bring yourself to go inside and pretend everything was fine.

Hopelessness doesn't always scream for attention. Sometimes it whispers in the quiet moments of our lives. Sometimes that whisper is just loud enough to wake you up and let you know that things aren't good right now, that things could be better, or that something might need to give in order for you life to get back on track.

What I Learned About Hope

For me, that awakening came slowly. I didn't have an immediate bounce back by listening to a podcast, meditating, or reading daily affirmations. I had to rebuild from the inside out, piece by piece. I had to go looking for the parts of myself I had left behind while trying to be everything for everyone else.

More than anything, I had to learn that hope wasn't something you stumbled upon or something that happened to you when life got better. Hope was something you built. Something you practiced. Something you became skilled at, especially when nothing else was working.

This understanding aligns with decades of psychological research. Dr. Shane Lopez, one of the leading researchers in hope theory, found that hope is not significantly related to native intelligence or income, but is consistently linked to academic achievement, career success, and overall life satisfaction.[7] More importantly, his research demonstrated that hope can be cultivated because it's not an inborn trait but a skill that can be developed and strengthened over time.[8]

That realization led me on a journey that took several years and eventually became the foundation for everything I'm going to share with you in this book. It's a process I've now used with dozens of colleagues, students, and friends who found themselves in similar places, whether they're burned out, disconnected, or going through the motions of a life that no longer felt like their own.

I'm not writing this as someone who "made it big" or figured out some secret formula for success. I don't really care about my social media following or getting the next promotion. I'm writing as someone who learned how to make life meaningful again, how to find purpose without losing yourself, and how to build hope even when the circumstances haven't changed much.

My background is in understanding how people learn and grow. I've spent nearly two decades leading in schools and in my community, coaching countless students and teachers through the challenges that shape their lives. I understand human development from both the research side and the trenches.

Most importantly, though, I understand living. I embrace the messy, ordinary, sometimes overwhelming business of building a life that matters when nothing feels easy.

If that's what you're after too, then the Pillars of Hope can help you find your way forward. Mastering each pillar is the goal, but mastering them is like mastering a language. There is no such thing as perfection. There is always work to be done, but that is part of the beauty of their design. You learn to live your life with hope because you start living your life with hope.

A Different Kind of Self-Help Book

This journey isn't going to be another list of seven steps to transform your life. It's not going to promise you'll feel better in thirty days or that positive thinking alone will solve your problems.

What I'm offering you is something more practical and more honest: a way of thinking about hope that treats it like the skill it actually is and a framework that gives you concrete ways to practice that skill every day.

Over the course of this book, we're going to walk through what I call the WE HOPE approach. The name isn't just because I love acronyms (I do), but because these six areas represent the foundational Pillars of Hope where hope gets built or threatened in real life.

Worth — Reconnecting with your value as a person
Energy — Protecting and directing your most precious resource
Habits — Creating change that lasts
Opportunity — Learning to see what's still possible
Perspective — Shifting how you see yourself and your situation
Edify — Finding meaning through connection and contribution

Picture these six skills as the columns of an ancient Greek temple. I've always been drawn to classical architecture. I am fascinated by the ruins of temples, pyramids, and cathedrals that have weathered centuries. There's something profound about how Greek temples were engineered. Each massive column bears an equal portion of the weight, and every pillar is essential to the structure's integrity. The solid ingenuity of these genius engineers created edifices that have endured millennia.

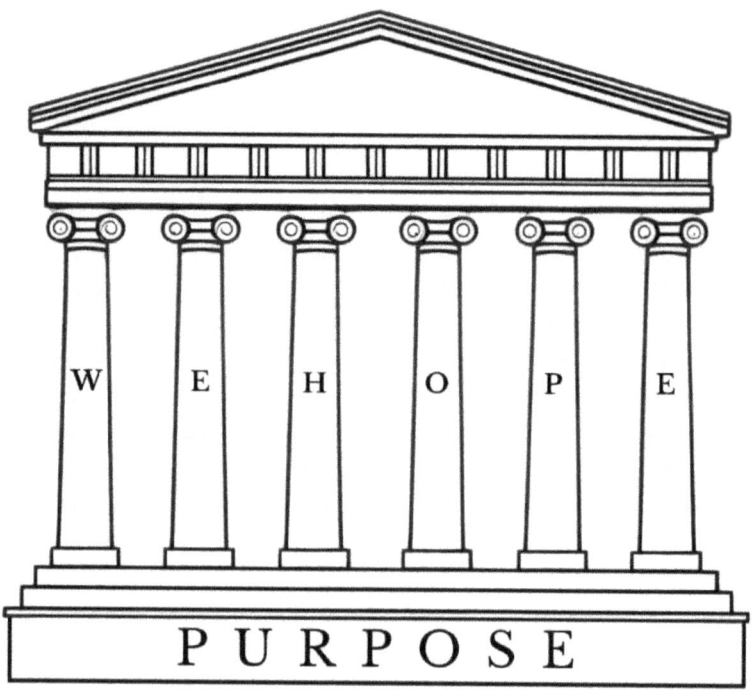

The WE HOPE framework works the same way. Each skill is substantial enough to be a monument in itself, requiring commitment and craftsmanship to master. The crucial part of the framework is that each column must work together to support the weight of a meaningful life. Remove one pillar, and the entire structure becomes unstable. Focus too intensively on just one or two, and you'll find the neglected areas eventually cause the whole system to falter. Each pillar must also be established upon the foundation of purpose, as will be noted throughout the book. Otherwise, the pillar might be strong on its own, but it couldn't withstand the constant barrage of hazards that could reduce the temple to rubble Most self-help approaches concentrate on individual pillars, which isn't wrong, but it's incomplete. If your goal is to build lasting hope, you need the full architectural foundation.

To help you craft a strong foundation for each skill, each chapter will give you both the why and the how. In addition, you will find stories that help you understand what's happening, insights that shift your thinking, and practical tools you can master the skill immediately.

Here's what makes this different from other approaches you might have tried, though. This book is designed to be your foundation, but it's not meant to be your only resource. Once you understand how hope works as a skill, you'll be able to apply it to the specific areas of your life that need the most attention.

That's why I've also created companion workbooks that take this same framework and make it practical for the challenges you're facing right now. Whether you're struggling with financial stress, career burnout, parenting overwhelm, or health and weight concerns, these guides walk you through applying what we hope for to your real life, with exercises, reflections, and action steps designed specifically for your situation.

You'll be able to choose one of these companion guides at no additional cost when you sign up at whatWEHOPEfor.com. Think of it as your first step toward taking what you learn here and making it work in the area where you need it most.

You don't need to believe in yourself fully right now. You don't need a five-year plan. You don't even need to feel "ready." You just need to be willing to take the next small step.

That's all hope really is, the next small step, taken with intention. Let's take it together.

Introduction to Stone Upon Stone

At the end of each chapter, you'll encounter the "Stone Upon Stone" section which is a carefully designed sequence that mirrors the ancient art of building pillars. Just as Greek columns were constructed with precision, starting from a solid foundation and rising through carefully placed stones to a magnificent capstone, your journey toward hope follows the same architectural principles.

Each Stone Upon Stone section is divided into three essential components. The **Base** provides your foundation through reflection and journaling exercises that help you examine your current state and clarify your understanding. Like the broad, stable foundation of a pillar, these reflective activities ground you in self-awareness and prepare you for growth. The **Column** represents the active work of elevating your skills to the next level. You will complete the challenges and practical exercises that build your skills stone by stone, strengthening your capacity in each area. Finally, the **Capstone** offers deeper resources and advanced learning opportunities that crown your efforts, providing the knowledge and tools that will protect everything you've built below and support the weight of what's to come.

Each activity is research-based and specifically designed to construct the pillar of hope within you. As you progress through each chapter, you're not just learning about hope, you're actively building it, crafting a structure within yourself that can weather any storm and support the life you're meant to live.

Stone Upon Stone – Building Your Pillar

Base

Connection Reflection:

Answer the following questions about your current reality.

- ° What part of my life feels disconnected right now? From myself, my purpose, or my hope?

- ° Give yourself permission to answer honestly. There's no judgment here, just awareness.

If it helps, complete this sentence:

"I'm starting to realize I've been pretending I'm okay with _____."

Column

Getting Started Challenge:

Pick one area of your daily life you can slow down and pay attention to for the next 24 hours.

Some ideas:

- ° How do you speak to yourself when you make a mistake?
- ° When do you feel most alive, even for a moment?
- ° How do you react to silence or stillness?
- ° Which pillars are you excited to work on?
- ° Which pillars are you anxious to start?

You don't have to fix anything yet. You're just observing where hope begins.

Capstone

Books:

Embracing Hope by Viktor Frankl

Option B by Sheryl Sandberg and Adam Grant

The Resilience Factor by Karen Reivich and Andrew Shatte

Podcasts:

FRIED. The Burnout Podcast

The Mel Robbins Podcast: "A Process for Finding Purpose: Do THIS to Build the Life You Want"

Lives Less Ordinary

Articles & Research:

"Hope Theory: A Member of the Positive Psychology Family" by Shane Lopez

"The Anatomy of Peace in Everyday Life" (Arbinger Institute)

"What We Get Wrong About Hope" (The Atlantic)

"The Neuroscience of Hope and Agency" (NeuroLeadership Institute)

Chapter Notes:

1. **Physical symptoms of disconnection**: Research in psychosomatic medicine consistently shows that emotional disconnection and chronic stress can manifest as unexplained physical symptoms. The mind-body connection is well-documented in studies of depression, anxiety, and burnout, where psychological states directly impact physical health through inflammatory responses and nervous system dysregulation.

2. **Epidemic of disconnection**: This terminology comes from multiple sources in public health and psychology literature. The concept has been formally recognized by major health organizations as a significant public health concern, with documented impacts on both individual and population health outcomes.

3. **Surgeon General's loneliness statistics**: From the U.S. Surgeon General's Advisory on the Healing Effects of Social Connection and Community (2023). Dr. Vivek Murthy's report documented that about one in two adults in America reported experiencing loneliness, leading to the formal declaration of loneliness as a public health epidemic.

4. **World Health Organization loneliness data**: The WHO reports that around 16% of people worldwide experience loneliness, as documented in their social determinants of health research. This represents approximately one in six people globally, making loneliness a significant international health concern.

5. **2024 loneliness study**: Data from the American Psychiatric Association's Healthy Minds Monthly Poll (2024), which found that 30% of American adults felt lonely at least weekly over the past year, while 10% reported feeling lonely every day. This study was conducted by Tulane University's School of Public Health and Tropical Medicine.

6. **Loneliness and mental health correlation**: Research from Harvard Graduate School of Education found that 81% of adults who were lonely also suffered with anxiety or depression compared to 29% of those who were less lonely, revealing the complex interconnections between loneliness, anxiety, and depression.

7. **Shane Lopez hope research**: Dr. Shane Lopez (1970-2016) was a senior scientist at Gallup and leading researcher in hope theory. His research found that hope is not significantly related to native intelligence or income but is consistently linked to school attendance, credits earned, academic achievement, and career success.

8. **Hope as a cultivatable skill**: Lopez's research demonstrated that hope can be measured, increased, and deployed as a skill. His work at Gallup showed that hope drives persistence, motivation, goal setting, and innovation, and that hopeful people are more successful, healthier, and happier than those who lack hope. Importantly, his research proved that hopefulness is not an inborn trait but can be cultivated and shared with others.

1: The Silent Crisis
When Hope Goes Into Hiding

"I'm not sure I can do this anymore," he said, almost out of nowhere. We were sitting in my classroom after school, surrounded by the familiar chaos of student work scattered across my desk and my chicken-scratch handwriting covering every available whiteboard space. The fluorescent lights hummed overhead, casting that particular institutional glow that made everything feel slightly surreal.

He had knocked on my door twenty minutes earlier, asking if we could talk. Something in his voice told me this wasn't about curriculum or classroom management.

He was a first-year teacher, about to finish the first semester of what should have been the beginning of a long career. His students loved him. I had seen it myself during classroom observations. They lit up when he walked into the room, eager to share stories from their weekend or show him drawings they had made. Parents requested his class specifically after hearing their children talk about the creative projects and the way he made his class feel exciting rather than a chore.

That day, though, he sat across from my desk, looking defeated in a way that seemed too heavy for someone so young and clearly gifted.

I was just starting out as an instructional coach at my school, which meant that on top of my own classroom assignments, I was any new teacher's go-to for support. I had spent over a decade teaching, weathering budget cuts and policy changes, surviving the kind of difficult years that either break teachers or forge them into something stronger. I thought I understood what it meant to struggle in this profession. I thought I had developed the wisdom to guide others through the rough patches that inevitably come.

Looking at this young teacher, I recognized so much of myself in his expression. I too had felt the pull to alter paths and do something else with my life many times throughout my career. There had been nights when I lay awake wondering if I was wasting my talents, if there was some other option that would feel more fulfilling, less exhausting, and let's be honest, more financially rewarding.

Through the self-doubt and personal challenges, I had learned something about hope during those difficult years. I had discovered that the feelings of doubt and disconnection weren't permanent, even when they felt overwhelming. I had found ways to reconnect with the parts of teaching that mattered most to me, to rebuild my sense of purpose when it felt lost.

With tears beginning to form in his eyes, he told me that teaching just wasn't for him. That all the work he had put into getting his degree, all the preparation and student teaching, had been someone else's dream and not his own. He spoke about family expectations and societal pressure to choose a "noble" profession, about how guilty he felt for wanting something different when there were so many people telling him he was exactly where he needed to be.

I didn't know what to say. Despite my years of experience, despite all the professional development sessions I had attended on supporting struggling teachers, I found myself at a loss for words. How do you respond when someone's pain is so raw and honest? How do you help someone see their value when they're convinced they don't belong?

I tried to help him see what I saw. His students rushing to greet him each morning, the careful way he explained difficult concepts, the patience he showed with the child who needed extra time to process instructions. I talked about the parent emails I had seen praising his communication, the way his classroom felt warm and welcoming to everyone who entered.

Even as I spoke, I realized I was trying to convince him of something he wasn't ready to hear. I was operating from my own experience, my own understanding of what it meant to find purpose in teaching, without really listening to what he needed.

This is where hope becomes critical, though I didn't have the language for it then. Hope doesn't get measured easily. It's measured by the lives you touch, the value you restore, the moments you create that no data can capture. However, hope also means having the courage to pursue the life that aligns with who you truly are, even when that choice disappoints others.

I wish I could say that I found exactly the right words that afternoon. I wish I could claim that I convinced this young teacher to see the light, to give teaching another chance, to discover the deep satisfaction that can come from this profession because that's how it worked out for me.

That's not how it worked out for this young teacher. Instead, I listened. I asked questions about his backup plan, about what kind of work made him feel energized rather than drained. I cried with him when he talked about feeling like a failure, when he described the shame he felt about wanting to leave. I sat with him in his uncertainty without trying to fix it or talk him out of it. I even gave him advice on how he should notify the principal.

A few short weeks later, he submitted his resignation and left mid-year. He never looked back.

That experience haunted me for months afterward. I questioned whether I had failed him, whether there was something else I could have said or done. I wondered if my own attachment to teaching had blinded me to other possibilities, if I had been too focused on keeping him in the profession rather than helping him find his authentic path.

That encounter, nevertheless, also planted a seed that would eventually grow into something larger. I began to see how many educators were struggling not just with the practical challenges of teaching, but with deeper questions about purpose and belonging. I started to recognize the patterns in the conversations happening in teacher workrooms and parking lots, the way so many of us were going through the motions without feeling truly connected to our work. Then, as I researched and prepared for helping teachers face these challenges, I noticed that the same issues educators faced were becoming more universal in our society, not just with issues we face in our careers. We have lost hope in so much of our lives. We no longer hope for a better financial future than our parents. We expect heartbreak out of romantic involvement. We struggle to see raising a family in a broken society. We don't have the will power or energy to work on being healthy in our eating and exercise habits.

My motivation for eventually developing what would become the WE HOPE model came partly from wanting to understand what had changed my own relationship with my career during those difficult years. I wanted to put into action the things that had helped me rediscover meaning and connection, so that I wouldn't be caught off guard again when working with other teachers who were considering leaving. As I realized these same struggles extended far beyond education and even careers, I began to see how the framework could help anyone who had lost hope in any area of their life.

The WE HOPE framework became more than just a tool for navigating difficult moments. It evolved into the foundation for building a life where hope isn't just something you turn to in crisis, but something you cultivate daily. When you understand hope and apply each pillar, hope becomes woven into the fabric of who you are. You begin developing the skills and mindset that allow you to face whatever comes with resilience and intention because of who you have become.

I want to be clear that I'm not judgmental of those who choose to leave education. The profession asks too much while providing too little support. The systemic problems are real and significant, and the job isn't a perfect fit for everyone. I still also believe that some teachers leave because they've lost touch with their sense of purpose and worth, not because teaching itself is wrong for them. I want those teachers to have the tools to reconnect with what drew them to education in the first place, so they can make their decisions from a place of clarity rather than despair, just like I want all people to have the same skills to overcome the obstacles they face.

The first step in rebuilding hope is learning the basics. That hope exists independent of your performance metrics, your promotions, or your follower count. That purpose and belonging are part of that equation. It means understanding that your value is inherent, not earned through achievement or approval.

I'm glad I stuck it out as a teacher through the hard times in my career. I'm proud of who I became and the lives I have been able to touch. However, I'm also proud of that young man who had the courage to seek out his authentic path, even when it meant disappointing people who believed he was meant to be a teacher. Sometimes honoring hope means staying and fighting for change. Sometimes it means having the courage to leave and find where you truly belong.

What Hope Isn't

Before we can fully understand what hope is and how to rebuild it, we need to recognize what we're actually dealing with when hope goes into hiding. The experience of losing hope often gets misunderstood or mislabeled, which makes it harder to address effectively. When we can name what hope isn't, we create space to discover what it actually is.

It's not depression, exactly, though it shares some of the same territory. It's not anxiety, though worry certainly lives there too. It's not grief in the traditional sense, though something important does feel lost.

It's more like a disconnection from the parts of life that used to matter. You start going through the motions of caring without actually feeling much of anything. You show up but you're not really present. You smile but it doesn't reach anywhere real.

I remember spending hours mustering up the slightest bit of energy to do the most menial of tasks. My entire life was on autopilot. I was too tired to do anything about it, and I didn't know where to find any of the answers. I wasn't just tired. I was somewhere else entirely, even though my body was still showing up and getting the work done. I wasn't living. I wasn't present, and when I got home, it didn't get better. It just got worse.

This kind of disconnection is more common than we admit. We live in a culture that celebrates being busy, productive, always on. When that pace becomes unsustainable, and it always does, we blame ourselves rather than questioning the system that demanded too much in the first place.

Now, my moments of hopelessness were triggered by career burnout, but there are many other catalysts for losing hope. For example, people frequently lose hope in their relationships, their finances, and their health.

The WE HOPE pillars are meant to benefit in each area where we struggle to find hope, and this framework can be used broadly to return to hope. In order to apply the framework in our lives, we need to better understand the hope we need to rebuild, but we can't understand what hope is until we understand what hope isn't. Hope's opposites and imposters can be dangerous, but naming them can help us avoid the pitfalls associated with them.

Hope's Opposites

One of the most effective techniques for learning and applying new vocabulary is through understanding the opposites of the term we are studying. Likewise, starting with a deep look at hope's opposites can lead to a more complete conception of hope and its applications.

First, cynicism feels safer than hope because it protects you from disappointment. It sounds sophisticated to say "I've seen too much to believe things can get better" or "People never really change." The problem is that cynicism becomes a self-fulfilling prophecy. When you expect the worst, you stop investing effort in creating something better. You end up creating the very outcomes you were trying to protect yourself from.

Cynicism masquerades as wisdom, but it's actually a form of intellectual laziness. It's easier to dismiss possibilities than to engage with the messy work of creating change. Cynics often pride themselves on their realism, but they're actually practicing a form of magical thinking that assumes the future is predetermined by the worst aspects of the past.

The cynic looks at a broken system and concludes that systems can't be fixed. The cynic looks at human failure and concludes that humans can't grow. The cynic looks at disappointed expectations and concludes that expecting anything good is foolish. In doing so, cynicism doesn't just predict failure; it actively works to ensure it by withdrawing the very effort that could create different outcomes.

Similar to cynicism, disbelief also has some varied nuance that makes it different from its hopeless cousin. Where cynicism expects the worst, disbelief simply refuses to accept that good things are real when they happen. It sounds reasonable to say "This is too good to be true" or "There must be a catch somewhere."

Disbelief protects you from being fooled, but it also prevents you from fully receiving positive experiences when they actually occur. You end up treating genuine opportunities, sincere compliments, or authentic connections as elaborate deceptions. The tragedy isn't that disbelief makes you suspicious of bad things. It's that it makes you suspicious of good things too.

When good things happen to the disbeliever, they're immediately dissected for hidden flaws or ulterior motives. A promotion is dismissed as temporary luck. A compliment is analyzed for sarcasm. An act of kindness is assumed to have strings attached. This constant vigilance against positive experiences creates a world where nothing good is ever quite real enough to be enjoyed.

Up next, despair and fear whisper that surrender is wisdom, that accepting defeat is simply being realistic about your limitations. It feels almost noble to say "I've tried everything" or "Some things are just impossible to change." Despair operates by convincing you that your current perspective is permanent and complete.

Fear doesn't just predict a bleak future. It actively works to create one by closing off the very pathways that could lead elsewhere. Fear paralyzes not just because it anticipates pain, but because it convinces you that avoiding pain is more important than pursuing anything meaningful. When fear becomes your primary advisor, you stop taking the risks that growth requires.

Despair takes temporary setbacks and reframes them as eternal truths. When you believe that failure is inevitable, you stop recognizing opportunities for different approaches, unexpected allies, or simply the way that time itself can shift the landscape of what's possible.

Of all of hope's opposites, apathy might be the most dangerous because it masquerades as peace. "I just don't care anymore" feels like relief after months or years of caring too much. Apathy isn't the absence of pain. It's the presence of disconnection. When you stop caring about outcomes, you also stop caring about your own growth, your relationships, your impact on the world around you.

Apathy promises rest but delivers numbness. It offers protection from disappointment by shutting down the capacity for engagement altogether. The apathetic person doesn't get hurt, but they also don't get to experience the full range of human experience that makes life worth living.

Hope's Imposters

The opposites of hope are easy to identify, but the imposters require a keen sense of self if we want to avoid them. In truth, the imposters aren't completely bad. They are usually effective for maintaining a "good" outlook on life. However, we need to recognize them for what they are and shift back into hope if we are to ever move past feeling stuck in our lives.

First, hope isn't the same as optimism. Optimism expects good things to happen. Hope is willing to keep moving even if they don't. Optimism looks at a difficult situation and assumes it will work out fine. Hope looks at the same situation and commits to doing what it can regardless of how things turn out.

Optimism can be brittle because it depends on external circumstances aligning with expectations. When things don't go well, optimism often collapses into its opposite. Hope is more durable because it's not dependent on outcomes being positive, only on the belief that engagement matters more than the results of that engagement.

Next, hope isn't toxic positivity. It doesn't require you to smile through pain or pretend everything's fine when it isn't. Real hope actually starts with honesty about where you are and what you're dealing with. Toxic positivity tries to skip over difficulty by focusing only on the bright side. Hope acknowledges the darkness while still choosing to light a candle.

Toxic positivity tells you to "just think positive" or "everything happens for a reason." Hope says "this is hard, and I'm going to keep going anyway." Toxic positivity invalidates real pain by insisting it shouldn't exist. Hope validates pain while refusing to let it have the final word.

Hope isn't passive faith either. It's not about waiting for someone or something else to fix your situation. Passive faith sits on the sidelines praying for rescue. Hope gets in the game and starts playing, trusting that its actions matter even when the scoreboard isn't clear.

The person operating from passive faith says, "I'll just wait and see what happens." The person operating from hope says, "I'll act on what I can control and adapt to what I can't." Hope is active by nature. It requires participation, not just observation.

What Hope Actually Is

What hope is, at its core, is the belief that you can influence your future through the choices you make today. Hope understands that you can't guarantee specific outcomes, but you can have confidence that any darkness you face will subside and open new opportunities to seek fulfillment. With hope, you learn to trust that your actions create possibilities that wouldn't exist otherwise.

Real hope is clear-eyed intent and action even in difficulty. It doesn't require rose-colored glasses or naive assumptions about how the world works. Hope sees problems clearly and chooses to engage with them anyway. It acknowledges uncertainty while refusing to let uncertainty become an excuse for inaction.

This kind of hope can be learned, practiced, and strengthened, regardless of your personality, your circumstances, or how hopeless you might feel right now.

Realizing that hope works more like a muscle than a mood changed everything for me. Feelings come and go. Motivation rises and falls. Skills can be developed through practice, regardless of how you happen to feel on any given day.

The psychologist Charles Snyder spent decades studying hope and found that it consists of three measurable components that include having goals that matter to you, being able to imagine pathways toward those goals, and believing in your ability to take action along those pathways.[1]

Goals - The "What" of Hope

Hope begins with clarity about what matters to you. Not what should matter, not what matters to other people, but what actually resonates with your deepest values and desires. These goals don't have to be grand or world-changing. They just have to be genuine.

The hopeful person doesn't necessarily have bigger dreams than anyone else. They have clearer ones. They've done the work of distinguishing between goals that come from external pressure and goals that emerge from the internal compass. They know the difference between what they want to achieve and what they think they should want to achieve.

Goals in the context of hope aren't rigid destinations. They're more like directions of travel. The hopeful person heading toward improved health doesn't fixate on a specific weight or measurement. They focus on the direction of becoming healthier. They know that the specific outcomes may vary, but the direction remains meaningful.

Clarity about goals also means accepting that you can't pursue everything at once. The hopeful person makes choices about where to invest their limited energy. They don't try to fix every problem or achieve every dream simultaneously. They pick what matters most right now and commit to moving in that direction.

Pathways - The "How" of Hope

Hope requires the ability to see multiple routes toward what matters to you. When one path gets blocked, hopeful people don't conclude that the destination is unreachable. They look for alternative routes.

This isn't about having a detailed plan for every contingency. It's about maintaining cognitive flexibility in the face of obstacles. The hopeful person knows that there are usually more ways to approach a problem than are immediately obvious. They've developed the mental habit of asking "What else could I try?" instead of "Why isn't this working?"

Pathway thinking is partly creative and partly practical. It involves both imagining new possibilities and learning from what others have done in similar situations. The hopeful person studies how other people have overcome similar challenges, not to copy their exact methods, but to expand their sense of what's possible.

People with strong pathway thinking don't get paralyzed by having too many options. They understand that you don't need to see the entire route to take the next step. They're comfortable with uncertainty about the distant future as long as they can identify the next meaningful action to take.

Agency - The "Why" of Hope

Agency is the belief that you have the capacity to make meaningful progress along the pathways you've identified toward the goals that matter to you. It's not confidence that you'll succeed at everything you attempt. It's confidence that your attempts matter and that you have the ability to learn and adapt as you go.

People with strong agency don't believe they can control outcomes, but they do believe they can influence them. They understand the difference between being responsible for results and being responsible for effort. They focus on what they can control while accepting what they can't.

Agency develops through experience of taking action and seeing that action create some kind of change, even if it's not the change you originally intended.

It grows stronger when you practice responding to setbacks as information rather than as evidence of your inadequacy.

The person with strong agency doesn't need to feel confident to take action. They understand that confidence often comes after action, not before it. They're willing to act on their best current understanding while remaining open to adjusting course as they learn more.

By establishing an understanding of these concepts, you can take your first steps towards building a life founded on hope. Follow those first steps and then take the time to reflect and apply as needed.

People Are Losing Hope in Modern Culture

Understanding hope as a skill helps explain why so many people feel hopeless in our current cultural context. We're living in conditions that actively undermine each component of hope.

Our goals get muddied by the constant noise of social media, advertising, and cultural messaging about what we should want. It becomes difficult to distinguish between authentic desires and manufactured ones. The sheer volume of possibilities presented to us creates decision paralysis rather than clarity about what truly matters.

Our pathways get obscured by the complexity of modern systems and the speed of change. The routes that worked for previous generations often don't apply to current challenges. Traditional institutions that once provided clear pathways forward have lost credibility or effectiveness, leaving many people uncertain about how to make progress on what matters to them.

Our agency gets eroded by systems that make individual action feel meaningless in the face of overwhelming challenges. Cultural shifts, economic inequality, political polarization, and technological disruption create problems that feel too big for any individual to address. When personal action feels insignificant, agency naturally weakens.

The culture itself often works against hope by promoting quick fixes over sustained effort, outcomes over process, and external validation over internal compass. We're encouraged to measure our worth by others' metrics by comparing outcomes that are largely outside our control while being given fewer opportunities to practice the kind of sustained, purposeful action that builds genuine agency.

This isn't abstract philosophy. It's practical psychology. The best part is that each of these components can be strengthened through intentional practice, even in the midst of cultural conditions that work against them. You, like many others, can use hope to counter the cultural pull to relinquish hope by spending the rest of our lives withering in meaningless filler.

Hope Isn't Lost — It's Hidden

If you're reading this feeling disconnected from hope, you need to know that you're not starting from zero. You're starting from experience.

Your life has already taught you things about what matters, what works, and what doesn't. Even in the midst of struggle, there have been moments, maybe small ones, when you felt more like yourself. Times when you acted with purpose, connected authentically with others, or simply felt present in your own life.

Those moments aren't accidents. They're clues. They point toward the parts of yourself that are still intact, still valuable, and still worth building on. Hope doesn't require you to become someone completely different. It asks you to become more fully who you already are.

Hope doesn't usually disappear in a dramatic moment. It fades gradually, the way daylight slips away on a winter afternoon, so slowly you don't notice until you're sitting in the dark. For me, it started with losing interest in things I used to enjoy. Books I'd been excited to read sat unopened. Weekend plans felt like obligations rather than opportunities. I stopped looking forward to much of anything, not because life was terrible, but because nothing felt particularly meaningful either.

Then came the disconnection from my own thoughts and feelings. I'd catch myself zoning out in conversations or forgetting what I'd been about to say mid-sentence. I started second-guessing decisions I would have made easily before, not because the stakes were higher but because I'd lost confidence in my own judgment.

The worst part was how normal it all looked from the outside. I was still teaching, still showing up to family dinners, still on the top of my game at work. I appeared to be holding it together, which meant I felt like I should be holding it together. The gap between how things looked and how they felt became another source of exhaustion.

This is what psychologists call "languishing." You're not thriving, not suffering, just existing in the space between. It's not acute enough to demand immediate attention; however, it's not sustainable either.[2] You can live there for a while, but you can't build anything meaningful from that place.

Understanding why hope goes into hiding helps explain why it can feel so difficult to access when you need it most. Hope retreats when it's not safe to be vulnerable, when the cost of caring feels too high, when the risk of disappointment outweighs the possibility of fulfillment.

Hope hides during times of overwhelming stress because it requires energy to maintain, and stress consumes the resources that hope needs to function. When you're in survival mode, your brain prioritizes immediate threats over long-term possibilities. The neural pathways that support hope get less attention when more urgent concerns demand your focus.

Hope also retreats in environments that punish vulnerability or penalize optimism. If you've been ridiculed for caring too much, criticized for being naive, or hurt by trusting in possibilities that didn't pan out, hope learns to stay quiet until it feels safer to emerge.

Sometimes hope hides because the world around you has become genuinely unsafe for the kind of openness that hope requires. If you're living in an abusive relationship, working in a toxic environment, or dealing with systems that punish authenticity, hope may withdraw as a form of protection. In these cases, hope isn't weak or broken. It's being wise by waiting for conditions that won't punish its presence.

Hope can also hide when the goals that once motivated you no longer fit who you're becoming. The career ambitions that drove you in your twenties might not resonate in your forties. The relationship patterns that worked when you were younger might feel inauthentic as you mature. When your old sources of hope no longer align with your current self, hope may withdraw until you can clarify what matters to you now.

Sometimes hope hides simply because you're exhausted. Physical exhaustion, emotional exhaustion, and mental exhaustion all make it harder to access the energy that hope requires. Hope involves looking beyond current circumstances toward future possibilities, and that kind of forward-thinking becomes difficult when all your resources are consumed by getting through each day.

The good news is that hidden things can be found. Hope that has retreated isn't hope that has been destroyed. It's hope that's waiting for the right conditions to emerge again. Creating those conditions doesn't require dramatic life changes or perfect circumstances. It requires small, consistent actions that signal to hope that it's safe to surface.

Hope begins to emerge when you start paying attention to moments when you feel more like yourself. These might be tiny moments. The first sip of coffee in the morning when you actually taste it. A conversation where you find yourself genuinely listening instead of just waiting for your turn to talk. A moment of appreciation for something beautiful you might normally walk past without noticing.

Hope surfaces when you begin to reconnect with what actually matters to you, separate from what you think should matter or what other people want you to care about. This process requires patience because authentic values often emerge slowly, especially if they've been buried under layers of external expectations.

Hope becomes visible when you start taking small actions aligned with those authentic values, even when you don't feel hopeful. The mother who's lost touch with joy but continues reading bedtime stories because connection with her children matters. The worker who's burned out but continues to treat colleagues with kindness because respect aligns with who they want to be. The person struggling with depression who still waters their plants because nurturing something alive feels important.

These actions might seem insignificant, but they're actually hope in disguise. They represent the continued belief that what you do matters, even when you can't feel that mattering directly. They're proof that hope hasn't disappeared but has simply gone underground, continuing to influence your choices even when it's not visible on the surface.

The framework I'll share with you in the coming chapters isn't about transforming your entire life overnight. It's about reconnecting with the foundation that's always been there, clearing away what's been covering it up, and building from that solid ground.

Hope isn't lost. It's just hidden under layers of exhaustion, disappointment, and disconnection that accumulated so gradually you didn't notice them piling up. Hidden things can be found. Once you know what you're looking for, the search becomes less overwhelming and more like coming home.

Stone Upon Stone – Building Your Pillar

Base

Present Moment Reflection:

Think about the last time you felt genuinely engaged with your own life, not performing or managing, actually present and interested.

- ◦ What was happening?
- ◦ What made that moment different?

Don't worry if it was small or seems insignificant. Pay attention to the quality of that experience, not its size or importance. As you reflect on this moment, notice what was different about your internal state.

- ° Were you focused on something outside yourself?
- ° Were you creating something?
- ° Were you connecting with another person or with something in nature?
- ° Were you using skills or abilities that felt natural to you?

Don't try to analyze these patterns or figure out how to recreate them perfectly. Simply notice them and write a few of the stories down to look back on later.

Column

Engagement Awareness Challenge:

For the next 24 hours, notice when you're going through the motions versus when you're actually engaged. You don't need to change anything. Just observe.

Some things to watch for:

- ° Conversations where you're actually listening vs. waiting for your turn to talk.
- ° Tasks you approach with curiosity vs. those you just want to get through.
- ° Moments when you feel like yourself vs. when you feel like you're playing a role.
- ° Physical sensations that accompany engagement vs. disconnection.
- ° Your relationship with time during different activities.

Don't judge what you observe. The goal is simply to develop awareness of your own patterns of engagement and disconnection.

Capstone

Books:

The Psychology of Hope by Charles Snyder

Hope for Cynics by Jamil Zaki

The Gifts of Imperfection by Brené Brown

Languishing by Corey Keyes

Podcasts:

On Being with Krista Tippett: "Hope in Hard Times" series

The Science of Happiness: "How Hope Can Help You Heal"

Ten Percent Happier: "The Neuroscience of Hope" with Shane Lopez

Unlocking Us with Brené Brown: "Hope vs. Despair"

Articles & Research:

"The Will and the Ways: Development and Validation of an Individual-Differences Measure of Hope" by Snyder et al.

"Languishing: The Neglected Middle Child of Mental Health" by Adam Grant (New York Times)

"Hope Theory: Rainbows in the Mind" by Shane Lopez (Psychology Today)

"The Science of Hope" (Greater Good Science Center, UC Berkeley)

Chapter Notes:

1. **Charles Snyder's hope theory**: Dr. C. R. Snyder (1944-2006) developed Hope Theory through decades of research at the University of Kansas. His work identified hope as consisting of three measurable components: goals (what you want to achieve), pathways (how you plan to achieve it), and agency (your belief in your ability to execute your plan). This framework has been validated across numerous studies and populations, establishing hope as a learnable skill rather than a fixed personality trait.

2. **Languishing research:** The concept of "languishing" was developed by sociologist Corey Keyes to describe the mental state between depression and flourishing. Research shows that languishing individuals experience low levels of emotional, psychological, and social well-being without meeting criteria for mental illness. This state affects productivity, creativity, and life satisfaction, and has become increasingly prevalent in modern society, particularly following major societal disruptions.

2: Building Hope
Your Foundation for Change

I spent a few years going back and forth trying to decide if I wanted to quit teaching. At one point, I sat in my empty classroom staring at motivational posters that felt like lies. After year eight of teaching, I had become a master of going through the motions while feeling completely disconnected from any sense of purpose.

Frequently, I would spend hours grading papers that students would glance at for thirty seconds before shoving into backpacks. I provided detailed feedback that would never be read, created lesson plans for students who seemed as disengaged as I felt, and answered emails from parents who saw me as an obstacle rather than an ally. The work that once energized me now felt like an elaborate performance where everyone was pretending it mattered.

Reflecting in that empty classroom, I realized I couldn't even remember why I had become a teacher in the first place. The idealistic twenty-four-year-old who had entered education to make a difference felt like a stranger. Somewhere along the way, I had lost the thread that connected my daily actions to anything meaningful.

At some point, I stumbled across a YouTube video by Simon Sinek. I couldn't get enough of his message. I don't know how many hours of clips I watched, but I was thirsting for a better way to get the most out of my life. I particularly connected with Sinek's work on finding your "why."[1] His approach wasn't about philosophical meditation or personality assessments. Instead, he asked people to identify specific moments when they felt most fulfilled and look for patterns across those experiences. I was desperate enough to try anything.

I started writing down memories from different periods of my life when I had felt genuinely engaged. I worked alongside a fellow teacher, James Sparks, who ended up being the cocreator of the WE HOPE Framework. We shared our stories and ignited something that had been missing for a long time.

As I collected these stories, a pattern emerged that surprised me. The moments when I felt most alive weren't about being in charge or being recognized. They were about creating conditions where other people could discover something about themselves they hadn't known before. I wasn't energized by teaching content as much as by helping people uncover their own confidence for understanding and applying their learning.

This realization shifted how I approached the upcoming school year. Instead of starting with curriculum standards and learning objectives, I decided to begin with purpose. If I was going to stay in teaching, I needed to reconnect with what made this work meaningful. More importantly, I suspected my students were struggling with the same disconnection I had been experiencing.

The first week of school, I introduced my classes to the same process I had used. Instead of the typical "get to know you" activities, we spent time identifying moments when they had felt most engaged and proud of their contributions. Initially, students were confused by questions that had nothing to do with academic subjects or career planning.

"Tell me about a moment when you lost track of time because you were so absorbed in what you were doing," I would prompt. "Describe a moment when you felt like you were being most authentically yourself." These weren't questions they were used to considering in school, and they definitely took some warming up enough to share these moments with one another.

Slowly, stories began to emerge. The quiet student who came alive when describing how she served in her church by making treats to share with the widows in her neighborhood. The goofball whose energy shifted to a serious tone when he talked about getting lost in his music performances. The athlete who spoke passionately about mentoring younger players rather than just winning games.

We looked for patterns in their stories just as I had done with mine. What kinds of problems naturally caught their attention? What activities made them feel energized rather than drained? When did they feel like they were using abilities that came naturally to them?

From these patterns, each student developed a personal purpose statement, a description of how they wanted to show up in the world. My understanding for each of them deepened, and I knew that I was on to something special. The students started to notice it too, and so we took some extra time to develop a purpose statement to govern the class.

The transformation in classroom culture was immediate and profound. Students began connecting academic content to their personal purposes. More importantly, they began showing up differently to their lives outside my classroom. They made choices based on their emerging understanding of what mattered to them rather than just following the path of least resistance. They started conversations about values and real learning instead of just grades. They approached challenges with curiosity rather than resignation.

What I discovered that year was that to connect to our purpose, we can't remain vague on what that purpose is. We have to recognize that purpose emerges when you pay attention to the consistent patterns in what energizes you across different contexts and time periods.[2] It reveals itself through engagement rather than contemplation.

The process we used that year became the foundation for everything I later developed about rebuilding hope. When students understood what genuinely mattered to them, they found energy for work that had previously felt meaningless. When they connected their daily actions to something larger than external expectations, they developed resilience for navigating obstacles that would have previously derailed them.

That classroom experiment taught me that hope and purpose are intimately connected. Hope without purpose becomes wishful thinking. Purpose without hope becomes grinding obligation. When they align, they create the foundation that makes sustained change possible.

The overarching aspects of the WE HOPE framework grew from that foundation of a year of watching students reconnect with what made their lives feel meaningful. WE HOPE is built on the understanding that hope isn't a feeling you wait for but a capacity you develop through consistent engagement with what matters to you.

Linking Hope and Purpose

Purpose isn't what you do for work. It's not your job title, your role in your family, or the way others describe you when you're not in the room. Purpose is the underlying pattern that connects your actions to something meaningful, the thread that runs through your choices when you're being most authentically yourself.

I used to think purpose was something you discovered through deep soul-searching or mystical revelation. I expected it to arrive like a lightning bolt of clarity, complete with detailed instructions and unwavering certainty. I waited for that moment through my twenties and into my thirties, growing increasingly frustrated as it failed to materialize.

Now, I know that purpose reveals itself through engagement, not contemplation. Purpose shows up in the work you lose track of time doing, the people you genuinely enjoy being around, the activities that feel like expressions of who you are rather than obligations you're fulfilling.

The connection between hope and purpose runs deeper than motivation. When hope and purpose align, they create something stronger than either could generate alone. Purpose gives hope direction and meaning. Hope gives purpose the energy and resilience to persist through difficulty. Together, they form the foundation that makes sustained change possible.

This alignment doesn't require perfect clarity about your life's mission or complete confidence about your direction. It requires enough connection to what matters to you that you can take meaningful action even when you're not sure where that action will lead.

Many people lose hope because they've become disconnected from any sense of purpose. They're functioning but not thriving, managing their responsibilities but not feeling particularly invested in the outcomes. They show up to their lives but don't inhabit them fully.

This disconnection often happens gradually. You start making choices based on what you think you should want rather than what actually resonates with you.[3] You begin measuring success by external standards rather than internal satisfaction. You find yourself living someone else's version of a good life while your own authentic desires get buried under layers of expectation and obligation.

The path back to hope requires reconnecting with what genuinely matters to you, separate from what you've been told should matter. This process can feel uncomfortable because it requires admitting that some of the choices you've made were based on other people's values rather than your own.

Sometimes the disconnection from purpose happens because life circumstances forced you to prioritize survival over authenticity.[4] You took the job that paid the bills rather than the one that excited you. You stayed in situations that were stable rather than fulfilling. You made practical choices that made sense at the time but gradually separated you from your deeper motivations.

There's no shame in having made survival-based decisions. The question isn't whether you've made perfect choices up to this point. The question is whether you're ready to start making choices that align more closely with who you're becoming rather than who you thought you should be.

Purpose isn't just about grand life missions or career paths. It shows up in how you treat the cashier at the grocery store when you're running late. It appears in whether you choose to listen deeply when a friend needs to talk or half-listen while scrolling through your phone. It emerges in small daily decisions about how you spend your time and attention.[5]

The person whose purpose involves creating beauty might express that through gardening, cooking, organizing their home, or simply noticing and appreciating beautiful moments throughout their day. The person whose purpose centers on problem-solving might find fulfillment in debugging code, helping friends work through relationship issues, or reorganizing systems at work to make them more efficient. When you're operating from purpose, even mundane tasks can feel meaningful because they're connected to something larger than themselves.

The reason hope without purpose fades becomes clear when you consider how many people achieve goals that were supposed to make them happy but find themselves feeling empty afterward. They got the promotion, bought the house, found the relationship, but none of it feels as satisfying as they expected. The external markers of success are there, but the internal sense of fulfillment is missing. Happiness is rarely found at the end of any road. You really can't procrastinate it.

This fading happens because we pursued (and oftentimes reached) goals where we misunderstood our purpose. In other words, we achieved things that looked good from the outside but didn't resonate with who we actually are inside. Without the anchor of genuine purpose, even significant accomplishments feel hollow.

Sitting With Discomfort

Reconnecting with authentic purpose requires developing tolerance for discomfort.[6] The process of figuring out what truly matters to you involves sitting with uncertainty, questioning assumptions you've held for years, and potentially disappointing people who have expectations about who you should be.

Most of us have been trained to avoid discomfort rather than work with it. Our default mode is to seek comfort, even at the cost of our own growth. We distract ourselves from difficult feelings, rush to fix problems before we understand them, or make premature decisions just to escape the tension of not knowing. This approach works fine for minor inconveniences but fails completely when dealing with meaningful life questions.

The discomfort you feel when examining your authentic desires isn't a sign that something's wrong. It's a sign that something important is trying to surface. That tension between who you've been and who you're becoming creates the energy necessary for lasting change.

Learning to sit with discomfort doesn't mean enjoying it or seeking it out unnecessarily. It means developing the capacity to remain present with difficult feelings long enough to understand what they're trying to tell you. It means getting comfortable with not having immediate answers to complex questions.

The difference between pressure and practice becomes important here. Pressure demands immediate results and perfect performance. It creates urgency around outcomes you can't completely control. Practice accepts that change best happens gradually through consistent effort over time.

When you approach self-discovery with pressure, you force answers that might not be ready to emerge yet. You try to shortcut the natural process of exploration and reflection that authentic purpose requires. This often leads to decisions that feel right temporarily but don't have staying power.

When you approach self-discovery as practice, you allow space for uncertainty while still taking meaningful action. You gather information through both reflection and experimentation. You make decisions based on your best current understanding while remaining open to adjusting course as you learn more.

One way to practice this is by doing exactly what James and I did so many years ago. You can start by using Simon Sinek's process for finding your why. I highly suggest you jump into his book listed in the Capstone of this chapter. The work there will provide a lot of clarity. As mentioned, the process starts with recalling moments when you felt genuinely proud of your contribution to something, times when you lost track of time because you were so absorbed in what you were doing, or instances when you felt like you were being most authentically yourself.

These don't have to be dramatic moments. They might be as simple as a conversation where you helped someone see their situation differently, a project where you solved a problem that had been bothering you, or a time when you organized something in a way that made life easier for others.

The key is identifying experiences where you felt energized rather than drained by your efforts, where the work itself felt rewarding regardless of external recognition. As you collect these stories, the next step is look for words that point toward your underlying motivations and values.

To date, we have done this exercise with individuals from all types of backgrounds, and I have yet to have an experience where I am disappointed by the process. This process requires patience because authentic purpose rarely reveals itself in a single session of self-reflection. It emerges gradually as you pay attention to what consistently draws your interest and energy across different contexts and time periods.

A main point of discomfort might come from realizing that your authentic purpose might not align with the path you're currently on, or with the expectations others have for your life. It can be unsettling to discover that what genuinely matters to you is different from what you thought it was supposed to be.

Sometimes the discomfort emerges because authentic purpose requires vulnerability. Living according to what truly matters to you means risking judgment from people who don't understand your choices. It means potentially disappointing family members, friends, or colleagues who have different ideas about what success should look like for you.

Other times the discomfort comes from recognizing that you've been living according to someone else's definition of a meaningful life. You might realize that you chose your career to please your parents, your lifestyle to impress your peers, or your goals to meet societal expectations rather than to express your authentic self.

This recognition can bring up feelings of grief for time. You might feel you've wasted your time or have regrets about choices you made for the wrong reasons.

These feelings are natural and important parts of the process of reconnecting with authentic purpose. They signal that you're moving from external validation toward your internal compass. You shouldn't shy away from such feelings. Recognize them for what they are and seek for ways to move past the discomfort and realize your purpose.

What Real Hope Looks Like

Real hope isn't the sanitized version you see in motivational posters or hear in graduation speeches. It's not about maintaining a positive attitude or believing that everything will work out fine. Real hope is grittier, more practical, and infinitely more useful than its cheerful imposters.

Hope that works when life is messy acknowledges that most meaningful changes happen slowly, with setbacks and detours along the way. It expects obstacles rather than being surprised by them. It plans for difficulty rather than hoping difficulty won't come.

This kind of hope understands that motivation comes and goes, but systems and habits persist. It relies more on structure than on feeling, more on consistency than on intensity. Real hope builds frameworks that work even when you don't feel particularly hopeful.

The mistake most people make is waiting to feel hopeful before taking action toward what matters to them. They treat hope as a prerequisite for change rather than a result of it. This approach keeps them stuck because hope isn't a feeling you can summon on command. It's a capacity you develop through practice.

The reason "trying harder" in a broken framework fails becomes clear when you understand that most people who feel stuck aren't lacking effort or commitment. They're applying tremendous energy to approaches that fundamentally don't work for their situation, personality, or values.

The person trying to force themselves to enjoy a career that doesn't fit them won't succeed by working longer hours or pushing through their dissatisfaction. The individual attempting to maintain a lifestyle that requires more resources than they have won't solve the problem by budgeting more carefully if the underlying structure is unsustainable.

The relationship that isn't working due to fundamental incompatibility won't improve through better communication techniques if the core issue is that the people involved want different things from life. Sometimes the framework itself is the problem, not the effort being applied within it.

Building hope as a skill means learning to act on your values even when you don't feel motivated to do so.[7] It means showing up for what matters to you consistently, especially when showing up feels difficult or unrewarding.

The mother who's struggling with depression but continues to read bedtime stories to her children is practicing hope. The worker who's burned out but still treats colleagues with respect is practicing hope. The person dealing with chronic illness who still takes care of their basic needs is practicing hope.

These actions might not feel hopeful in the moment, but they represent the continued belief that what you do matters, even when you can't feel that "mattering" directly. They're proof that hope operates below the level of conscious awareness, continuing to influence your choices even when it's not visible on the surface.

Moving from exhaustion to alignment requires understanding that exhaustion often comes from swimming against your own current rather than from working too hard.[8] When your daily actions consistently conflict with your values, energy gets depleted faster than it can be replenished.

The person who values creativity but spends all their time on administrative tasks will feel drained even if the work isn't particularly demanding. The individual who craves solitude but works in a highly social environment will feel exhausted even if they enjoy the people they work with. The misalignment itself is what creates the fatigue.

Moving toward alignment doesn't necessarily require dramatic life changes. Sometimes it means finding ways to incorporate your values into your current situation. Sometimes it means making gradual shifts toward roles, relationships, or environments that better support who you're becoming.

WE HOPE provides a different approach. Instead of trying to force change through willpower alone, it creates conditions that make positive change more likely to emerge and sustain itself over time.

The Pillars of Hope of Worth, Energy, Habits, Opportunity, Perspective, and Edify each address a different aspect of what it takes to rebuild hope and create lasting change in your life. You can work through them as a linear process, but the Pillars are interconnected with one another, with hope, and with purpose, creating the beautiful structure that is a life worth living.

Another unique tidbit about the acronym is that we are reminded of the reconnective nature of the framework with the word "WE" at the beginning. What are "we" hoping for? This journey isn't to be taken alone. You have to reconnect with yourself, with your values, with your impact, and with a community.

Let's break down each pillar for a moment before you really establish a firm understanding with the following chapters.

Worth involves recognizing that your inherent value is separate from your achievements or others' opinions. You have worth and you are worthy.

Energy focuses on protecting and replenishing your physical, mental, emotional, and spiritual resources.

Habits build systems that support your goals without requiring constant decision-making.

Opportunity trains your attention to notice possibilities that exhaustion and hopelessness make invisible. It teaches us to seek growth with an eye toward the future.

Perspective brings us back to the present. It helps you reframe current challenges in ways that reveal options rather than confirming limitations. We see ourselves, our circumstances, and our obstacles in a new light.

Edify connects you to something larger than yourself through service to others. It's your true application of purpose.

The Pillars work together to create a foundation strong enough to support meaningful change over time. They address the root causes of hopelessness rather than just its symptoms. They build capacity for sustained action rather than relying on temporary bursts of motivation.

What makes this framework particularly powerful is that it has an all-encompassing nature. With that, I mean that all of your future learning will help strengthen at least one of the Pillars. With so many theories of "self-help" and suggestions for improvement, it might be easy to get lost and frustrated knowing even where to start. What is one to do? Give up? No, now that you've found hope, start there. Take your experiences and all your knowledge, and use them to build your temple.

As I study others' works on personal improvement, I rarely find a new nugget of wisdom that conflicts with WE HOPE, and it's exciting to learn theories and ideas and identify where they fit and align within the framework. The Capstone sections of each chapter are just that, my connections to the multitude of theories that help each of us get the most out of life.

One more thing to note about application. While my initial crisis of hope centered around career burnout, I've successfully applied these same principles to rebuild hope in my health fitness, my familial relationships, and my finances as well.

When I was struggling with chronic health issues that doctors couldn't quite diagnose, I used the Worth component to stop defining myself by my symptoms. Energy helped me identify which activities genuinely restored me versus those that depleted me, even when they seemed healthy on paper. Habits allowed me to build sustainable wellness practices that didn't require perfect motivation every day. Opportunity opened my eyes to treatment options and lifestyle changes I'd been too overwhelmed to consider. Perspective helped me reframe my health challenges as information rather than evidence of personal failure. Edify connected me to others dealing with similar issues, which both helped them and reminded me that my struggles could serve a purpose beyond my own healing.

The framework proved equally powerful in building my family relationships when I realized that years of career stress had created distance between me and the people I loved most. Worth reminded me that my value as a husband and father wasn't tied to my professional achievements or ability to provide perfectly. Energy helped me recognize that I was investing my best emotional resources at work and bringing home whatever was left, leaving my family with my depleted self. Habits allowed me to create consistent rituals for connection that didn't depend on having energy or feeling motivated after long days. Opportunity opened my eyes to small moments for meaningful interaction that I'd been too distracted to notice. Perspective helped me see family conflicts as opportunities for deeper understanding rather than evidence of my failures as a parent or spouse. Edify reminded me that modeling the Pillars of Hope to demonstrate growth and vulnerability for my children was one of the most important ways I could serve their development.

The same framework transformed my relationship with money when financial stress was creating anxiety that affected every area of my life. Did I mention I raised a family of six on a single teacher income for 13 years of my career? Worth helped me separate my value as a person from my net worth or earning capacity. Energy revealed how financial worry was draining resources I needed for creative and strategic thinking about solutions. Habits enabled me to build financial practices that supported my goals without requiring constant willpower. Opportunity helped me notice income possibilities and expense reductions. Perspective allowed me to view financial challenges as puzzles to solve rather than evidence of personal inadequacy. Edify turned me into a financial literacy missionary. For a while, I couldn't stop preaching to everyone I knew about the miraculous benefits of budgeting and compound interest. I even took time during my homeroom classes at school to discuss the benefits of investing in mutual funds at an early age

Whether you're struggling with relationships, health, finances, career dissatisfaction, or a general sense that life isn't working the way you hoped it would, these six Pillars of Hope provide a comprehensive approach to a satisfying, joyful, and effective life.

Are You Ready to Begin?

Readiness for change doesn't usually feel the way most people expect it to. It doesn't arrive with fanfare or complete certainty. It usually shows up quietly, as a subtle shift from "I can't do this" to "I wonder what might happen if I tried."

Readiness isn't about having all the answers or feeling completely prepared. It's about reaching a point where the discomfort of staying the same becomes greater than the discomfort of trying something different. It's about being tired enough of your current situation that you're willing to risk the uncertainty that comes with change.

Many people wait for perfect conditions before beginning anything meaningful. They want to feel completely ready, have all the resources they need, and be confident about the outcome before they take the first step. This approach ensures they never begin because perfect conditions never arrive.

What readiness actually means might surprise you. It's not about confidence or clarity or having your life ready and organized. Readiness is simply the willingness to start where you are with what you have, knowing that you'll figure out the rest as you go.

Readiness looks like accepting that you don't need to have everything figured out before you begin making changes. It's the recognition that waiting for perfect timing or ideal circumstances is actually a form of avoidance. It's understanding that the best time to plant a tree was twenty years ago, but the second-best time is now.

Sometimes readiness emerges from exhaustion with your own excuses. You realize that you've been using the same reasons to avoid change for months or years, and those reasons are starting to feel stale even to you. The story you've been telling yourself about why change isn't possible begins to sound less convincing.

Other times, readiness comes from a growing awareness that time is precious and finite. You become less willing to spend years living someone else's version of your life or settling for less than what's possible for you. The urgency isn't panic but clarity about what deserves your limited time and energy.

The paradox of readiness is that you become ready by beginning, not the other way around. You develop the capacity for change by practicing change, even in small ways. You build confidence by taking action, not by thinking about taking action.

The courage to start before you feel ready comes from understanding that no one ever feels completely ready for meaningful change. The people who create the lives they want aren't the ones who waited until they felt confident. They're the ones who acted despite uncertainty, who started with what they had rather than waiting for what they thought they needed.

I definitely don't want you to be reckless or make any major life changes without any consideration. I just want you to distinguish between reasonable preparation and perfectionist delay tactics. Recognize when you're using the need for more information or better conditions as an excuse to avoid the discomfort that comes with any genuine attempt at growth.

If you made it this far and continue reading, you're already demonstrating a form of readiness. You've recognized that something needs to change, and you're seeking tools to make that change possible. That recognition and that seeking are evidence that hope is still active in your life, even if it might not feel particularly strong right now.

The willingness to keep looking for solutions when previous attempts haven't worked is itself a form of hope. The commitment to understanding your situation more deeply rather than just accepting it as permanent shows that some part of you still believes change is possible.

The framework ahead requires commitment but not perfection. It asks for consistency but not intensity. It works with your life as it currently is rather than demanding dramatic upheaval. Are you ready?

Stone Upon Stone—Building Your Pillar

Base

Purpose Statement Development:
Collect 3-5 specific stories from your life when you felt most fulfilled and energized. These should be moments when you lost track of time, felt genuinely proud of your contribution, or experienced a sense of authentic engagement.

For each story, write down:

- ° The situation: What was happening? Who was involved?
- ° Your role: What specifically were you doing or contributing?
- ° The feeling: How did you feel during and after this experience?
- ° The impact: What effect did your actions have on others or the situation?

After collecting your stories, look for patterns by asking:

- ° What kinds of problems or challenges naturally drew your attention?
- ° What activities made you feel energized rather than drained?
- ° When did you feel like you were using abilities that came naturally to you?
- ° What themes or values appear across multiple stories?

Take time to develop a purpose statement that resonates with you.

Column

Purpose In Action Challenge:

Using the purpose statement you developed in the Base exercise, commit to finding moments where you can live your purpose over the next 48 hours.

- ° If your purpose involves helping others discover their capabilities, offer genuine encouragement to someone who's struggling with self-doubt.
- ° If your purpose centers on creating order or beauty, organize or beautify one small space in a way that serves others.
- ° If your purpose involves problem-solving, identify one issue in your immediate environment and take action to address it.
- ° If your purpose focuses on connection, initiate a meaningful conversation with someone you care about

Consider the following guidelines for your actions:

- ° It should be specific and observable (not just a mental shift).
- ° It should connect to your purpose statement in a way that feels authentic to you
- ° It should be something you can do without changing up your routine.

After taking your purposeful actions, reflect and document the following:

- ° How did it feel to act from your sense of purpose rather than obligation?
- ° What resistance or discomfort did you notice, and how did you work with it?
- ° What was the impact on yourself and others?
- ° How might you incorporate more purpose-driven actions into your regular life?

Capstone

Books:

Start with Why by Simon Sinek

Daring Greatly by Brené Brown

Drive: The Surprising Truth About What Motivates Us by Daniel Pink

The Purpose Driven Life by Rick Warren

Podcasts:

On Being with Krista Tippett: "Finding Purpose in Uncertain Times"

The Tim Ferriss Show: Episodes on finding purpose and meaning

Ten Percent Happier: "Working with Difficult Emotions"

The School of Greatness: "Discovering Your Purpose" episodes

Unlocking Us with Brené Brown: "Living Into Our Values"

Articles & Research:

"How to Find Your Purpose in Life" (Greater Good Science Center, UC Berkeley)

"The Science of Purpose" by Kendall Cotton Bronk

"Sitting with Discomfort: A Practice Guide" (Mindful Magazine)

"The Connection Between Purpose and Hope" (Psychology Today)

"Why Discomfort Is Necessary for Growth" (Harvard Business Review)

Chapter Notes:

1. **Simon Sinek's "Find Your Why" process**: Sinek's methodology involves identifying specific stories from your life when you felt most fulfilled, then analyzing these experiences to discover common themes that point toward your underlying motivations and values. His research demonstrates that people with a clear sense of purpose are more resilient, motivated, and successful across multiple life domains. The process focuses on moments of authentic engagement rather than external achievements or recognition.

2. **Purpose emergence through engagement:** Psychological research supports the idea that purpose develops through active exploration rather than passive reflection. Studies in positive psychology show that purpose crystallizes when individuals pay attention to activities that create flow states, align with personal values, and generate intrinsic rather than extrinsic motivation.

3. **Disconnection from authentic values:** Research in self-determination theory demonstrates that when people make choices based on external expectations rather than intrinsic motivation, they experience decreased well-being, reduced resilience, and increased susceptibility to anxiety and depression. This phenomenon is particularly pronounced in cultures that prioritize external validation over personal fulfillment.

4. **Survival-based decision making:** Maslow's hierarchy of needs provides the theoretical framework for understanding how people prioritize basic security over self-actualization when resources are limited. However, recent research suggests that individuals can pursue both

survival and authenticity simultaneously through creative problem-solving and gradual life adjustments rather than dramatic overhauls.

5. **Purpose in daily interactions:** Research from the University of Michigan shows that people who connect routine activities to larger purposes experience greater life satisfaction and demonstrate increased resilience during challenging periods. This principle applies to interactions as simple as grocery store encounters, which can become expressions of values like kindness, patience, or community connection.

6. **Tolerance for discomfort in growth:** Studies in developmental psychology confirm that meaningful personal growth requires what researchers term "optimal anxiety" – enough discomfort to motivate change without overwhelming the individual's coping capacity. The ability to sit with uncertainty while continuing to take meaningful action is a key predictor of successful life transitions.

7. **Framework integration research:** Meta-analyses of self-help and personal development interventions show that the most effective approaches integrate multiple evidence-based components rather than relying on single techniques. Frameworks that address both internal factors (values, mindset) and external factors (habits, environment) produce more sustainable outcomes than approaches focusing on only one dimension.

8. **Misalignment and energy depletion:** Occupational psychology research demonstrates that value-work misalignment is a primary predictor of burnout, even when job demands are manageable. Individuals whose daily activities conflict with their core values show elevated cortisol levels, decreased immune function, and increased rates of anxiety and depression, regardless of external measures of job success.

Part 2

The Six Pillars of Hope

3: W - Worth
You Are Not Broken

Lucius Quinctius Cincinnatus and Harland Sanders have almost nothing in common except that you might not even recognize their names. One was a Roman farmer who became dictator of the ancient world's greatest empire in 458 BCE. The other was a Kentucky gas station owner who became the face of fried chicken in 1952. Cincinnatus wielded absolute power over legions and senators. Sanders wielded a pressure cooker and eleven herbs and spices. Cincinnatus saved Rome from military annihilation. Sanders saved dinner plans with his secret recipe. The Roman returned to his plow after sixteen days of supreme command. The Colonel spent decades getting rejected by restaurants before anyone would serve his chicken.

The only thing these two men shared was that everyone around them completely underestimated what they were capable of. When it came down to it, each demonstrated that they understood the Pillar of Worth just as well as any individual could.

When Rome faced a major military crisis in 458 BCE, the senators didn't want to appoint Cincinnatus as dictator. They saw a simple farmer who spent his days behind a plow, lacking the sophistication and political connections that supreme command required. What could a man who worked the soil possibly understand about leading armies and managing an empire? Cincinnatus, however, knew something about himself that the Roman elite couldn't see. He understood that practical leadership and moral authority were exactly what Rome needed. The approach from the Senate was to apply more of the same, more political maneuvering from the same people who had created the crisis in the first place.

Once Cincinnatus convinced enough leaders of his approach, it took only sixteen days to restore order and halt the crisis. He defeated Rome's enemies, organized the government, and then in a surprising and noble act, voluntarily gave up absolute power to return to farming. The senators who had dismissed him as inadequate watched in amazement as he walked away from the ultimate prize that they would have killed for. Cincinnatus knew his worth wasn't determined by political titles or public recognition.[1] His value came from his character and capability, and those existed whether Rome and its Senate acknowledged them or not.

Nearly 2,500 years later, Harland Sanders faced his own version of dismissal. At age 65, after failing at dozens of careers, he was told by restaurant owner after restaurant owner that his chicken recipe was nothing special. They saw a washed-up old man with white hair and a folksy manner trying to peddle fried chicken to establishments that already knew how to cook. What could a former gas station operator possibly teach professional restaurateurs about food?

Sanders knew something about his recipe that the restaurant industry couldn't taste. He had spent years perfecting a pressure-cooking method and spice blend that created something genuinely different. More than 1,000 rejections didn't shake his confidence in what he had created.[2] He knew the worth of his product existed independent of whether anyone else recognized it. When someone finally said yes, KFC became a global empire, not because Sanders had suddenly become worthy of success, but because he had finally found a means to turn his vision into reality.

I spent years trapped in my own version of this story, particularly around advancing in my career. For the outsider, hiring practices in public schools are a unique spectacle. Changes in positions and job openings are oddly predictable. Each spring, school districts across the country post their openings for the upcoming year. Rarely do opportunities open up outside of this small hiring window. If you don't land the job you hope to get, you have to wait an entire year before you get to apply again.

Each spring brought new administrative positions where I hoped to get hired and advance my career. Each year, I prepared my resume, got out my suit, and practiced my interviewing skills ad nauseum. I knew I had the skills and competence to do the job well, but year after year, I would be notified that it wasn't my run to be promoted yet and to be patient. After what felt like my hundredth interview, I found myself reading yet another "we've decided to go with another candidate" email. This one stung more than the others because the interview had felt different and the position was at the school where I dreamed of working. The interview questions had led to conversation that flowed naturally. The panel had even laughed at my jokes, and I had walked out feeling cautiously optimistic for the first time in years.

When that familiar rejection arrived, I didn't just feel disappointment, but I felt an odd validation, and not in a good way. I felt validated in my growing belief that I simply wasn't administrator material, that I was fundamentally lacking something essential that the more qualified candidates possessed. The voice in my head said, "*See? You were fooling yourself again. They could tell you don't have what it takes.*"

After a few years of spring hiring cycles where precious few positions opened up to fields of 50, 60, sometimes 100 applicants, I had stopped seeing these rejections as competitive mathematics and started seeing them as personal verdicts. Each "no" had become evidence that I was inadequately prepared, insufficiently connected, or missing some critical quality that others naturally possessed.

My inner critic convinced me that truly other candidates didn't face this many rejections, that everyone else had some combination of skills, experience, or relationships that I would never develop. I started approaching interviews not with confidence in my abilities, but with desperate hope that somehow I could convince them I was worthy despite my obvious inadequacies.

At some point, I realized I had been carrying this voice's assessment of my worth into every interview, every conversation, every attempt to advance. I wasn't just competing against other candidates. I was competing against my own internalized beliefs that I didn't deserve to win. Unlike Cincinnatus, who knew his capabilities even when Roman senators couldn't see them, or Sanders, who trusted his recipe despite 1,000 rejections, I had accepted other people's inability to recognize my worth as evidence that it didn't exist.

What I had to learn was what both Cincinnatus and Sanders either learned or understood intuitively. Worth isn't determined by external validation or comparative rankings.[3] Your value as a person exists independent of whether others can recognize it, whether opportunities align with your timeline, or whether you measure up to impossible standards that keep shifting just out of reach.

The Roman farmer knew he could lead before the senators acknowledged it. The Kentucky Colonel knew his recipe was extraordinary before any restaurant would serve it. Their worth wasn't created by their eventual success. Their success became possible because they recognized the worth that had been there all along.

The Pillar of Worth is about reclaiming that same understanding for yourself. Worth is the first Pillar because we all need to be reminded that worth is inherent in being human before we can go forward and act as humans. You are not a problem to be solved before you can be worthy of good things. You are a person with inherent value that exists independent of external recognition, competitive outcomes, or perfect performance. Once you understand this distinction, everything changes about how you approach your goals, your relationships, and your daily experience of being alive.

Rewriting Your Story

There's a kind of heaviness that comes when you don't just feel tired or lost but you feel **unworthy**. The voice in your head doesn't always say things like "*I hate myself.*" Sometimes it sounds like

"*I don't bring anything valuable to the table.*"
"*I'm falling behind.*"

"Everyone else seems to be handling life better than I am."
"What's the point of trying if I always end up back here?"
These thoughts might seem casual, even logical, but over time, they start to chip away at your identity. They whisper that your value is tied to your performance, that your worth is conditional, that if you're not producing, achieving, or pleasing someone, you don't really matter.

For me, the voice started quietly, the way these voices tend to do. It began with small observations that felt reasonable enough. *"You should have handled that better." "Other people seem to manage these things more easily." "Maybe you're not as capable as you thought."*

The voice grew louder with each disappointment, each mistake, each moment when life didn't unfold the way I'd imagined it would. It began rewriting the story of who I was, replacing confidence with questions, replacing self-respect with endless second-guessing. By the time I recognized what was happening, the voice had become so familiar I mistook it for truth.

Self-worth erodes in layers, like paint peeling from an old house. First, you lose faith in your judgment. Decisions that once felt natural become sources of anxiety. You start seeking validation from others for choices you used to make easily, not because the stakes are higher but because you no longer trust your own perspective.

Then you lose faith in your capabilities. Tasks that used to energize you become evidence of your inadequacy. A project that doesn't go perfectly becomes proof that you're not good enough. A relationship that requires effort becomes confirmation that you're too difficult to love. Every challenge transforms from an opportunity to grow into a test you're failing.

Finally, you lose faith in your fundamental worth as a person. You start believing that your value depends entirely on your performance, your productivity, your ability to meet external standards that keep shifting just out of reach.[4]

This erosion can happen so gradually that by the time you notice it, the damage feels permanent. You look in the mirror and see someone broken, who requires fixing before they can be worthy of good things. You assume that everyone else can see what you see, that your inadequacy is as obvious to them as it is to you.

The cruelest part of losing self-worth is how it masquerades as realism. The voice convinces you that you're finally seeing yourself clearly, that you were naive to think you deserved better. It frames self-criticism as honesty and trains you to believe that self-compassion is delusion. You start believing that being harsh with yourself is the same as being responsible, that accepting your worth is the same as making excuses.

Looking back at my moments of falling short of those promotions, what made them so devastating wasn't just another rejection, but it was recognizing how completely I had accepted the voice's narrative about my worth.

Rebuilding self-worth after setbacks requires understanding that worth isn't earned through achievement or lost through failure. Your value as a person exists independent of your performance in any particular area of life. This isn't positive thinking or feel-good psychology. This is recognizing a fundamental truth that gets obscured when we're struggling.

You are a person navigating complex circumstances with limited information and imperfect tools, doing the best you can with what you have available. The setbacks you've experienced don't define your capacity for future success. They define your experience, and experience becomes wisdom when you're willing to learn from it rather than be crushed by it. Every mistake contains information about what doesn't work, which brings you closer to discovering what does.

Your struggles don't make you less worthy of love, respect, or opportunity. They make you human. The people worth connecting with understand this because they've faced their own struggles. The opportunities worth pursuing are ones that allow for growth and learning, not ones that demand perfection from the start.

The most important thing to understand about this internal voice and the stories it tells is that it isn't telling you the truth about who you are. It's telling you a story based on fear and past hurt in a misguided attempt to protect you from future pain. The voice sounds so much like your own thoughts that you assume it must be reliable, but volume doesn't equal validity.

This internal narrator operates like an overprotective parent who's so afraid of you getting hurt that they convince you never to try anything risky. The voice highlights every failure while conveniently forgetting your successes. It magnifies your weaknesses while minimizing your strengths. It treats temporary setbacks as permanent character flaws.

The voice also feeds on incomplete information. It makes sweeping judgments based on limited perspective, drawing conclusions about your entire worth from isolated incidents. One rejected job application becomes "*nobody wants to hire me.*" One relationship that didn't work becomes "*I'm unlovable.*" One mistake becomes "*I always mess everything up.*"

Learning to question this voice rather than automatically believing it changes everything. Just because you think something doesn't make it true. Just because a thought feels familiar doesn't make it accurate. Just because your internal critic speaks with confidence doesn't mean it knows what it's talking about.

The solution isn't to silence the voice completely, which is usually impossible anyway. The solution is to recognize it as one perspective among many, not the final authority on your worth or potential. You can acknowledge the voice without being controlled by it, notice its patterns without being defeated by them.

When you catch the voice rewriting your story in ways that diminish your worth, pause and ask yourself what a caring friend would say about the same situation. Ask what advice you'd give someone else facing identical circumstances. Ask what evidence exists that contradicts the voice's harsh assessment.

Reclaiming self-worth begins with noticing the voice that's been narrating your failures and recognizing that critic for what it is. This voice may have developed to protect you from future disappointment by lowering expectations, but it's created a different kind of suffering by cutting you off from your own potential.

The Highlight Reel Trap

In addition to your inner voice becoming your own personal critic, social media has turned comparison into a full-time occupation.[5] We scroll through carefully curated highlights of other people's lives and measure them against the unedited reality of our own experience. We see their successes without their struggles, their breakthroughs without their setbacks, their finished products without their messy process.

This constant exposure to everyone else's best moments creates an impossible standard. We start believing that everyone else has figured out something we're missing, that they're naturally more capable, more organized, more fulfilled than we are. We assume their lives are as smooth as their posts make them appear.

The comparison trap is particularly devastating when you're already struggling with self-worth. When you're questioning your own value, other people's apparent success becomes evidence of your inadequacy. Their achievements highlight your setbacks. Their confidence emphasizes your uncertainty. Their apparent ease makes your effort feel pathetic.

What we don't see in those curated glimpses are the moments of doubt, the failed attempts that came before the success, the support systems that made achievements possible, the privileges and opportunities that created advantages, the struggles that continue even after public victories.

We don't see the successful entrepreneur's years of rejection and near-bankruptcy. We don't see the happy couple's difficult conversations and moments of disconnection. We don't see the confident speaker's anxiety before taking the stage or the fulfilled parent's moments of complete overwhelm.

Comparing your inside experience to someone else's outside appearance will always leave you feeling inadequate because you're comparing incomparable things. You know all your own struggles, doubts, and failures. You know none of theirs.

Even comparing actual outcomes misses the point because outcomes depend on countless variables beyond individual effort or worth. Two people can work equally hard and get completely different results because of timing, resources, connections, luck, or circumstances beyond their control.

The person who gets promoted might have had access to mentorship or networking you didn't receive. The person who seems to have effortless relationships might have learned communication skills from parents who modeled them well. The person who appears naturally confident might have grown up in an environment that consistently affirmed their worth.

This doesn't diminish their achievements or suggest that outcomes are entirely random. It means that outcomes are never accurate measures of personal worth or even effort. Focusing on comparisons distracts you from the only things you can actually control, which are your own choices and responses.

Comparison also assumes that there's a single definition of success that applies to everyone. It ignores the reality that what fulfills one person might drain another, that what challenges one person might bore another, that what feels meaningful to one person might feel empty to another.

The life that looks perfect to you might feel imprisoning to the person living it. The achievements you envy might have come with costs you wouldn't be willing to pay. The path that worked for someone else might lead nowhere meaningful for you because you're different people with different values, strengths, and circumstances.

Breaking free from comparison requires shifting focus from outcomes to process, from results to effort, from external measures to internal compass. The relevant question isn't "*How am I doing compared to them?*" but "*Am I moving toward what matters to me?*" The next question that follows should be "*Am I learning and growing from my experiences?*"

Your worth isn't determined by ranking yourself against others on some imaginary scoreboard. Your worth exists independent of how you measure up to external standards. You can celebrate other people's success without it diminishing your own value. You can acknowledge your own struggles without them proving your inadequacy.

Permission to Be Yourself

One of the most damaging myths about personal growth is that you need to earn the right to improve your life by first proving you're worthy of better circumstances.[6] This backwards logic suggests that you must demonstrate worthiness through suffering, struggle, or perfection before you deserve to pursue what you want.

This myth creates a trap where you postpone taking care of yourself until you've somehow proven you deserve care. You delay pursuing meaningful goals until you've demonstrated worthiness through achievement. You withhold self-compassion until you've earned it through flawless performance.

The truth is exactly the opposite. Your fundamental worth as a person is what makes you worthy of change, growth, and better circumstances. You don't earn worth through achievement. You pursue achievement because you're already worthy of a fulfilling life.

This understanding shifts the entire framework for personal change. Instead of trying to fix what's broken about you, you're developing what's already valuable. Instead of earning the right to be happy, you're claiming what already belongs to you. Instead of proving your worth through external validation, you're acting from inherent worth toward external goals.

Recognizing your inherent worth doesn't mean believing you're perfect or that you don't need to grow. It means understanding that your capacity for growth is itself evidence of your value. Broken things don't grow. Worthless things don't develop. Your ability to learn, change, and improve proves your worth rather than earning it.

This perspective protects you from the toxic cycle of shame-based motivation. When you try to improve yourself from a place of believing you're fundamentally flawed, every setback becomes evidence of your brokenness. Every mistake confirms your inadequacy. Every moment of struggle proves you don't deserve better.

When you approach change from a place of inherent worth, setbacks become information rather than indictments. Mistakes become learning opportunities rather than character judgments. Struggles become part of the growth process rather than evidence that you should give up.

When I was struggling to advance in my career, I had to learn to ignore the drive to advance temporarily. I had to get back to the present. I had to recognize that even though I wasn't advancing at the pace I thought I should be, I needed to reconnect and re-anchor to my work as a classroom teacher. I had value and worth in that arena, and I needed to make the most of the time I was going to get in that season of my life.

Understanding your worth also protects you from trying to become someone else in the name of improvement. The most sustainable changes are ones that align with who you already are rather than forcing you to deny your nature.

Being unapologetically yourself doesn't mean refusing to grow or change. It means growing and changing in directions that honor what's authentic about you rather than trying to conform to external expectations of who you should be.

Your personality traits, values, strengths, and even what some people call weaknesses are not mistakes to be corrected. They're the raw material you have to work with. The goal isn't to become someone different but to become more fully yourself. When you stop trying to *prove* your value and start *honoring* it, you become someone who no longer abandons yourself to be accepted by others.

The introvert doesn't need to become an extrovert to have meaningful relationships. They need to find ways of connecting that honor their need for depth and quiet processing. The sensitive person doesn't need to become tough to survive difficult circumstances. They need to learn how to protect their sensitivity while still engaging fully with life.

Your natural inclinations, when developed and applied skillfully, become your greatest strengths. Your challenges, when understood and worked with rather than against, often point toward your most important areas of growth.

Authenticity isn't about doing whatever you feel like doing without consideration for others or consequences. It's about aligning your actions with your values and purpose, expressing yourself in ways that feel genuine, and pursuing goals that resonate with who you actually are rather than who you think you should be.

This alignment creates sustainable motivation because you're working with your nature rather than against it. Changes that honor your authentic self feel like coming home rather than forcing yourself into an uncomfortable costume.

Being unapologetically yourself also means accepting that not everyone will understand or appreciate who you are, and that's not a problem to solve. Trying to be acceptable to everyone requires denying so much of yourself that you end up acceptable to no one, least of all to yourself.

The people who matter will appreciate your authenticity, even when it's inconvenient or challenging. The opportunities that are right for you will be enhanced by your genuine engagement rather than diminished by it.

Aligning to Your Purpose

Once you begin separating your worth from your achievements, you may find yourself asking a deeper question. If your value isn't tied to what you produce or accomplish, then who are you underneath all of that?

This is where a sense of purpose can offer clarity, the kind that anchors you in something steadier. Purpose in this sense is not dramatic or flashy. It is quiet and steady. It reminds you who you are when life feels chaotic or uncertain. It brings you back to yourself when comparison, pressure, or fear begin to pull you in other directions.

When you're not connected to this internal anchor, it becomes easy to drift. You might say yes to things you don't care about because you want to be seen as reliable. You might take on responsibilities out of guilt rather than intention. You might move through your days fulfilling roles instead of living a life that reflects your actual values.

When that happens, your decisions start to feel disconnected from who you are. The work you do might be fine on the outside, but it doesn't feel meaningful on the inside. The goals you're chasing might look impressive, but they no longer feel personal. This is the subtle erosion that happens when you lose alignment with your core.

Reconnecting with purpose doesn't require a total life overhaul. It begins with remembering what truly matters to you. Often, the clues have been there all along. They show up in the moments when you feel most alive, most grounded, or most proud. These moments shine like a guiding star because something true came through.

In the previous chapter, you were asked to reflect on the moments when you feel most like yourself. Now, consider how those moments help realign your worth. Think about the qualities that consistently show up in your decisions, even when no one is watching. Reflect on the kind of person you admire and what that says about your values. Consider the times in your life when you felt proud of how you showed up. Maybe the outcome wasn't perfect, but in these moments you know that your actions reflected something real about your worth.

As you reflect on these patterns, new themes might begin to surface now that you've had time to reflect on purpose and worth. You might notice that presence matters more to you than perfection. You might realize that honesty, compassion, or growth show up again and again. These aren't just preferences. They are pieces of who you are.

Having a purpose statement that reflects these values can help you stay connected to that sense of direction and that sense of worth, a statement that grounds you when life feels noisy. Something you can return to when self-doubt creeps in or when the expectations of others start to drown out your own voice.

Examples might sound like:

I want to move through life with quiet courage and steady truth.
I am at peace when I stay rooted in love and honesty.
I am here to grow, to care, and to live in alignment with what matters.

Even when I feel uncertain, I can return to what I value.

This sentence doesn't need to be eloquent. It just needs to resonate with you. You can revise it over time as you learn more about yourself, your purpose, and your worth. What matters is not how poetic it sounds but how honest it feels.

Once you've identified your purpose, it can become an inner compass to provide personal direction. When you're making decisions, pause and ask whether the choice brings you closer to or further from what you value. When you're unsure how to respond to a situation, return to that sentence and let it help you decide how to show up.

The more you align with it, the more peaceful your choices will begin to feel. You may notice you feel less pressure to prove yourself and more clarity about where to focus your time. You may find yourself saying no to what drains you and yes to what sustains you, not because someone else said it was okay, but because you are listening to your own truth.

This kind of alignment doesn't eliminate struggle, but it gives the struggle meaning. You know why you're doing what you're doing. You know who you are becoming through the process. That knowledge is what keeps you grounded when everything else feels uncertain.

Five Commitments for Big Changes

Knowing your purpose means you can align life to it, but the sort of self-respect that comes with living your purpose isn't built through grand gestures or dramatic life changes. It's built through small, consistent actions that demonstrate to yourself that you matter enough to take care of.

These practices work because they create evidence of your worth through your behavior. When you consistently treat yourself with care and consideration, you begin to internalize the message that you deserve care and consideration. When you follow through on commitments to yourself, you rebuild trust in your own reliability.

The most important daily practice for rebuilding self-respect is keeping small promises to yourself. These don't need to be major, life-changing resolutions. They need to be specific, manageable commitments that you can complete consistently.

The first commitment to your worth is to take better care of your physical body. Something simple like keeping a promise to drink a full glass of water when you wake up builds the same self-trust as keeping a promise to exercise for an hour every day, but it's much more achievable when you're starting from a place of depleted worth. The size of the promise matters less than your ability to keep it.

Physical care translates directly into emotional well-being because your body and mind are connected in ways that become obvious when you start paying attention. Taking a shower when you don't feel like it, choosing foods that nourish rather than just fill you, getting enough sleep even when staying up feels more appealing, all send messages to your unconscious mind about your worth.

This is about treating yourself with the same consideration you'd show someone you care about. You wouldn't let a good friend skip meals, ignore their health, or neglect their basic needs. You deserve the same level of care from yourself.

Second, setting and maintaining boundaries is another essential commitment for building self-worth. Boundaries aren't walls that keep people out. They're guidelines that protect what's important to you while allowing for meaningful connection with others.

A boundary might be as simple as not checking email after a certain time in the evening, saying no to commitments that don't align with your priorities, or asking for what you need in relationships rather than hoping others will guess.

Boundaries require practice because they go against cultural messages that suggest your worth comes from your usefulness to others.[8] Learning to disappoint people when necessary protects your energy for what matters most and demonstrates that you value your own well-being.

Next, speaking to yourself with kindness rather than criticism is perhaps the most challenging but important commitment for rebuilding self-worth. The voice in your head that provides commentary on your actions, decisions, and experiences has enormous influence over how you feel about yourself.

Most people would never speak to a friend the way they speak to themselves. The internal dialogue is often harsh, critical, and focused on failures rather than efforts. Changing this requires conscious effort to notice the voice and intentionally choose different words.

This doesn't mean lying to yourself or pretending mistakes don't matter. It means speaking about mistakes the way you'd speak about them to someone you were trying to help rather than someone you were trying to punish.

I had to change the stories I was telling myself. I learned to be my own best friend instead of my harshest critic. I had to learn how to encourage myself, be kind to myself, believe in my worth, and live my purpose without expecting the world to provide me the avenues to live that purpose. I recommitted to my students in the classroom. I stopped focusing so much on the chatter of whose turn it was to be promoted. I worked on mentoring the teachers around me, and I decided that I could be a leader with or without a title assigned to me. Each day, I got to be me, and I got to find new ways to live my purpose, and I learned to enjoy and celebrate those moments as they happened. I noticed them happening more and more often, and it eventually led to me falling in love with teaching again.

With that, celebrating small wins is the next commitment that rebuilds self-worth by training your attention to notice progress rather than just problems. Most people are quick to notice what goes wrong and slow to acknowledge what goes right. This creates a distorted view of reality that emphasizes failure over success.

Intentionally acknowledging moments when you handle something well, make progress toward a goal, or simply show up when it would be easier not to, helps balance your internal narrative. These celebrations don't need to be elaborate. Simply noticing and appreciating your own efforts is enough.

Finally, engaging in activities that align with your values, even in small ways, is an essential commitment. This commitment reinforces your sense of worth by connecting your daily actions to what matters most to you. If creativity is important to you, spending ten minutes sketching or writing honors that value. If connection matters, reaching out to a friend demonstrates care for what you prioritize.

These value-aligned actions work even when they don't produce obvious results because they reinforce your identity as someone who lives according to their principles. They create coherence between who you are and how you behave, which is the foundation of self-worth.

The key to all these commitments is consistency rather than intensity. Doing something small every day builds more self-respect than doing something big once a month. The daily repetition creates new patterns of thinking and behaving that gradually replace the old ones.

Start with one or two commitments that feel manageable given your current circumstances. Build consistency with those before adding others. The goal is to create sustainable changes that last rather than dramatic changes that fade out after a few weeks.

Self-worth can grow slowly, but it grows surely when you're consistent about treating yourself with care. Every small action that honors your worth contributes to a foundation that becomes stronger over time.

In the end, my changes in how I viewed my own worth led to me being so much better at living in the moment and being a better version of myself than if I had been promoted earlier in my career. Eventually, I did get the opportunity to advance into the administration side of education. Instead of instant validation of my worth, I had to start all over again. I had recommit to value my worth in this new arena. I again had to overcome my personal narrative that led to imposter syndrome, fear of failure, and unforeseen challenges.

Worth, as a Pillar of Hope, can be like that, but it has to be at the forefront of your foundation, or the rest of the WE HOPE framework cannot be effective.

Revisit this Pillar often. Realign to your purpose. Recommit to your worth. Remember to celebrate *being* and *becoming* you. With worth, purpose, and hope as your foundation, you will have the motivation required to build the energy to thrive.

Stone Upon Stone—Building Your Pillar

Base

Self-Worth Assessment:

Complete this evidence-based self-assessment to understand your current relationship with worth. For each statement, rate yourself on a scale of 1-5 (1 = never true, 5 = always true):

1. I believe I deserve good things in my life, regardless of my achievements
2. When I make mistakes, I speak to myself with kindness and understanding
3. I can acknowledge my strengths without feeling like I'm being arrogant
4. My sense of worth doesn't depend on other people's opinions of me
5. I set boundaries that protect my well-being, even when it disappoints others
6. I celebrate small wins and progress, not just major accomplishments
7. I can receive compliments without immediately deflecting or dismissing them
8. I trust my own judgment, even when others disagree
9. I take care of my physical and emotional needs consistently
10. I believe I have inherent value as a person, separate from my performance

Reflection Questions:
- Which statements scored lowest for you? What patterns do you notice?
- Think of a recent moment when you felt genuinely proud of yourself (not for achieving something, but for how you showed up). What was happening?
- Complete this sentence honestly: "I would feel more worthy if I could stop believing that _____."
- When is your inner critic loudest? What triggers the harsh voice in your head?

Column

The Worth Evidence Challenge:
For the next seven days, you'll actively collect evidence of your inherent worth through three specific practices:

Days 1-2: The Inner Voice Audit Track your self-talk for 48 hours. Every time you notice critical self-talk, write it down. Then, rewrite each critical statement as if you were speaking to a good friend facing the same situation. Notice the difference in tone and content.

Days 3-4: Commitments Practice Choose one small, manageable commitment to yourself each day (drink water upon waking, take three deep breaths before checking your phone, write down one thing you're grateful for). Take note of how it feels to be reliable to yourself.

Days 5-7: The Values Alignment Action Identify one core value from your purpose reflection. Each day, take one small action that expresses this value. For example, if you value kindness, offer genuine encouragement to someone. If you value growth, spend ten minutes learning something new. If you value authenticity, express one genuine opinion or feeling.

Daily Documentation: Each evening, write brief answers to:
  ° How did I honor my worth today?
  ° When did I feel most like myself?
  ° What evidence did I create today that contradicts any negative beliefs about my value?

End-of-Week Reflection:
  ° What surprised you about this exercise?
  ° Which practice felt most natural? Most challenging?
  ° How might you continue building evidence of your worth beyond this week?

Capstone

Books:
  Self-Compassion by Kristin Neff
  The Confidence Code by Kay and Shipman
  The Self-Confidence Workbook by Markway and Ampel

You Are a Badass by Jen Sincero

Podcasts:

The Self-Compassion Podcast with Christopher Germer

Therapy for Black Girls: "Building Self-Worth"

The Life Coach School Podcast: "Self-Worth vs. Self-Confidence"

Dear Sugars: "The Truth About Self-Worth"

Articles:

"The Development and Validation of a Scale to Measure Self-Compassion" by Kristin Neff

"Why You Should Stop Being So Hard on Yourself" (Harvard Business Review)

"The Science of Self-Compassion" (Greater Good Science Center)

"How to Build Lasting Self-Worth" (Psychology Today)

Chapter Notes:

1. **Intrinsic vs. extrinsic worth research:** Studies in self-determination theory demonstrate that individuals who derive their sense of worth from internal values and personal growth show greater psychological resilience and life satisfaction compared to those who rely primarily on external validation such as titles, recognition, or comparative achievements.

2. **Persistence and entrepreneurial success:** Research on entrepreneurial psychology shows that successful business founders often face significantly more rejections than failures before achieving breakthrough success. Studies indicate that persistence in the face of repeated rejection is one of the strongest predictors of eventual entrepreneurial success, independent of initial skill level or market conditions.

3. **Self-worth stability research:** Psychological studies demonstrate that individuals with stable self-worth (i.e. a worth that doesn't fluctuate based on external circumstances) show better mental health outcomes, more resilient responses to setbacks, and greater willingness to take healthy risks in personal and professional development.

4. **Performance-based self-worth consequences:** Research in clinical psychology shows that individuals who tie their self-worth primarily to performance outcomes experience higher rates of anxiety, depression, and burnout. This pattern is particularly pronounced in high-achievement environments where external standards continuously escalate.

5. **Social comparison and social media impact:** Studies from the American Psychological Association demonstrate that frequent social media use correlates with increased social

comparison behaviors, which in turn predict higher rates of depression, anxiety, and decreased life satisfaction, particularly among individuals already struggling with self-worth issues.

6. **Growth mindset and self-compassion research:** Carol Dweck's research on growth mindset, combined with Kristin Neff's work on self-compassion, shows that individuals who approach personal development from a place of inherent worth rather than earned worthiness demonstrate more sustainable behavior change, greater resilience during setbacks, and improved overall psychological well-being.

7. **Mind-body connection in self-care:** Neuroscientific research confirms that physical self-care practices directly impact emotional regulation and self-perception. The vagus nerve, which connects the brain to major organs, responds positively to intentional physical care, creating measurable improvements in mood, stress response, and self-worth indicators.

8. **Boundary-setting and psychological health:** Research in interpersonal psychology demonstrates that individuals who maintain clear, consistent boundaries report higher levels of self-respect, lower rates of resentment in relationships, and better overall mental health outcomes. Boundary-setting behavior also correlates with increased feelings of personal agency and control.

4: E - Energy
Protect Your Fuel

One of my colleagues went through a period that can only be described as taxing. For Bryan, everything seemed to pile up simultaneously. Young children demanded constant attention and energy, straining his marriage to the breaking point. Financial pressures mounted while work demands intensified. Meanwhile, the activities that once brought him joy, particularly his love for sports and competition, became distant memories he couldn't afford in terms of time, money, or energy. He felt trapped in a cycle where giving everything to others left nothing for himself.

For nearly two years, Bryan carried this weight. He functioned, but barely. The breaking point came during what should have been an ordinary evening at home. He realized that he and his wife hadn't shared a single positive interaction in over a week. Every conversation centered on logistics, problems, or conflict. In that moment, the weight of his exhaustion crashed down on him completely. He told me about his meltdown. He had to go hide from his family because he didn't want them to see what he was experiencing right there in his living room. He had finally concluded that he couldn't continue living this way. How could he find the energy to keep at it?

Years earlier, I had gone through something similar, a common pattern for so many of us in this modern era. My wife has countless pictures of me sleeping in the most random places, and while she found it amusing, these images tell a deeper story. During one family outing to our favorite mountain park, we had just finished a peaceful picnic lunch when the kids ran off to play. Instead of joining them, I felt an overwhelming wave of exhaustion that I couldn't fight. I quietly slipped away to our car, reclined the front seat, and was unconscious within minutes. My wife tracked me down and snapped a photo of me there, completely spent in the middle of what should have been a rejuvenating family day.

For nearly a decade of my life, when people asked if I was okay, I would respond with a quick "just tired." Looking back, I realize that phrase had become my shield. I had legitimate reasons for exhaustion such as being a young father early in my career, working multiple side jobs to make ends meet. Nevertheless, that phase represented something far deeper than ordinary fatigue.

"Just tired" often serves as code for something more complex. Regular tiredness improves with rest. What I was experiencing needed to be rebuilt, and I needed to understand where my energy was disappearing.

Initially, I tried every conventional approach to restore my energy. I examined my daily routines and realized I was completely disconnected from my physical presence. My mind constantly churned through problems, lesson plans, financial calculations, and career strategies because those seemed like the responsible things for a man to focus on. However, this mental hyperactivity was draining me in ways I didn't understand.[1]

My persistent exhaustion eventually led to feelings of depression, prompting me to seek professional help. When I first described my symptoms to my doctor, he immediately suggested I might be clinically depressed. I went home and shared this assessment with my wife, who asked a crucial question: "Do you think you're depressed, or does this feel like something else?" I told her that while something was clearly wrong, depression didn't quite capture what I was experiencing, and the depressive cloud that hung over me was completely out of character. The only way that I can describe it is that I knew that something was just off.

She encouraged me to insist on more comprehensive testing. The doctor relented and ordered some additional tests. Those tests revealed that I was dealing with a significant hormone imbalance requiring medication. Additionally, despite being at a healthy weight and having no obvious risk factors, we found that I was suffering from severe sleep apnea.[2] Once we addressed these underlying medical issues, my energy returned not just to previous levels but beyond what I had experienced in years.

Because I had navigated my own energy crisis, I was uniquely positioned to help Bryan when he reached his breaking point. We started with purpose and worth, but those foundations weren't sufficient on their own. These foundations were definitely beneficial, but Bryan still felt like his life was wilting. We moved to the next phase of his development. The Pillar of Hope that Jared needed to build most urgently was Energy. Interestingly, while my situation had required medical intervention, Bryan's path to restoration was more straightforward but not any less challenging to put into practice.

We began with basic energy management principles, and remarkably, these fundamental changes were enough. Bryan had been sacrificing so extensively to "support" those around him that he had depleted his reserves completely. The key breakthrough came when we identified ways he could simultaneously support others while reinvigorating himself. He started taking bike rides around the neighborhood with his older children, which eventually evolved into mountain biking adventures together. He and his wife committed to watching one movie together each week, creating sacred time for their relationship. Once Jared discovered how to be a support others in ways that energized rather than drained him, he was ready not just to survive but to thrive.

So far, you should have used this book to set the foundation for hope. We've done a lot of reflection and thought exercises. The Pillars of Energy and Habit, however, are where daily action will be required if you want to thrive. Keep in mind that we can't disentangle the Pillars of Energy and Habits. Building habits requires energy, and maintaining energy requires consistent habits. Remember this interconnection as you approach the daily work of the next two chapters and identify and implement your plans for rebuilding hope in your life.

Your Most Valuable Resource

When most people think about making changes in their lives, they focus on time management, goal setting, or motivation. They create elaborate plans and detailed schedules, assuming that organization, better planning, or some expert's system will carry them through. What they often miss is the most fundamental resource required for any meaningful change: energy.

Energy isn't just about feeling tired or alert. It's the fuel that powers every decision you make, every conversation you have, every task you complete, and every moment of presence you offer to the people and activities that matter to you. Without adequate energy, even the best plans become overwhelming burdens rather than exciting possibilities.

The problem is that energy operates differently than other resources. Time is finite and measurable. Money has clear boundaries and visible limits. Energy is more subtle, more complex, and far more personal. What energizes one person might drain another completely. What restores you on Tuesday might exhaust you on Thursday, depending on what else is happening in your life.

Most people treat energy as if it's unlimited or as if managing it is a luxury they can't afford. They push through fatigue, ignore their body's signals, and assume that willpower alone should be enough to sustain them through anything. This approach works temporarily, but it creates a deficit that compounds over time.[3]

When your energy is consistently depleted, everything becomes harder. Simple decisions feel overwhelming. Tasks that used to be routine require enormous effort. Relationships that used to feel supportive start to feel demanding. Goals that once excited you begin to seem impossible.

Operating without enough fuel for the life you're trying to live is almost standard procedure in our busy cultures. When our bodies do finally decide to reject our pace of life, we oftentimes resort to binging or addictive behaviors to cope. Such behaviors simply open the door to more shame, pain, and guilt over our perceived laziness, procrastination, or flawed efforts. Just as a car won't run efficiently on an empty tank, you can't function effectively when your energy reserves are depleted.

Understanding energy as a finite resource that needs to be protected and replenished changes how you approach everything. Instead of trying to power through exhaustion, you start paying attention to what drains you and what restores you. Instead of assuming you should be able to handle anything, you begin making choices based on your actual capacity rather than your ideal capacity.

This shift requires letting go of the cultural myth that being constantly busy equals being productive or valuable. It means recognizing that rest isn't earned through exhaustion but required for sustained effectiveness. It means treating your energy with the same respect you'd give any other precious resource.[4]

The people who seem to accomplish the most while maintaining their well-being aren't superhuman. They've learned to work with their energy rather than against it. They understand their own patterns, protect their capacity, and make strategic choices about where to invest their limited fuel.

Learning to manage your energy isn't about becoming more efficient or productive, though those might be side effects. It's about honoring the reality of being human in a world that often demands more than humans can sustainably give. It's about creating space for hope to flourish by ensuring you have the energy to nurture it.

Reconnect Body and Mind

Modern life creates an artificial separation between physical and mental experience that doesn't exist in reality.[5] We treat the body as a vehicle for the mind, something to be managed and controlled rather than listened to and cared for. This disconnection costs us enormously in terms of both energy and well-being.

Your body holds information that your mind often misses or dismisses. Physical tension might be the first sign that a situation isn't right for you, appearing long before your conscious mind recognizes the problem. Fatigue might indicate emotional overwhelm rather than just physical tiredness. Restlessness might signal a need for change that your logical mind hasn't yet acknowledged.

When you're disconnected from your body, you miss these early warning signals. You push through discomfort that's trying to tell you something important. You ignore fatigue that's protecting you from burnout. You override instincts that could guide you toward better choices.

This disconnection also makes it harder to access the body's natural capacity for restoration and resilience. Your body knows how to release tension, process emotions, and restore energy, but these processes require your attention and cooperation. When you're constantly in your head, you miss opportunities for the kind of integrated healing that happens when mind and body work together.

Physical practices that reconnect you with your body's wisdom don't need to be complicated or time-consuming. The following practices can help you restore the natural partnership between your physical and mental experience. Each one is designed to be accessible and immediately actionable, requiring no special equipment or extensive time commitment.

1. Breathe with Awareness Simple awareness of your breathing throughout the day helps bridge the gap between mental activity and physical presence. Try taking three conscious breaths whenever you transition between activities, noticing how your breath naturally deepens when you pay attention to it.

2. Release Tension Consciously Noticing areas of tension in your body and consciously releasing them creates space for energy to flow more freely. Do a quick body scan several times a day, starting from your head and moving down to your feet. When you find tension, breathe into that area and imagine it softening.

3. Move for Pleasure, Not Punishment Movement that feels good rather than punishing helps restore the natural partnership between body and mind. This might be gentle stretching, walking without a destination, dancing to music you love, or any activity that allows you to **inhabit your body with pleasure rather than just efficiency.**

4. Practice Nurturing Touch Touch is another powerful way to reconnect with your physical self. This might mean taking baths that soothe your skin, wrapping yourself in soft fabrics, getting massages when possible, or simply placing your hands on your heart when you're feeling disconnected or overwhelmed.

5. Eat with Body Wisdom Eating in a way that honors both nutrition and pleasure helps heal the split between body and mind. This means paying attention to how different foods make you feel, eating when you're hungry and stopping when you're satisfied, and choosing foods that nourish you rather than just filling time or numbing emotions.

6. Create Sacred Sleep Rituals Sleep becomes more restorative when you approach it as a collaboration between mind and body rather than just a biological necessity. Creating rituals that help both your mind and body prepare for rest, paying attention to what helps you sleep well, and treating sleep as sacred time rather than wasted time all contribute to better energy.[6]

7. Ground Yourself in Nature Spending time outdoors, even briefly, helps restore your connection to your physical self and the larger rhythms of life. This might mean feeling grass under your bare feet, sitting with your back against a tree, or simply stepping outside and taking five deep breaths of fresh air when you feel disconnected.[7]

This list of suggestions is not exhaustive, and you can find many other practices with a quick internet search. The final outcome of these practices, however, isn't for you to develop an unhealthy obsession with your body or every physical sensation, nor would I like you to dismiss the importance of keeping your connection to your mind through thoughtful reflection and the development of your mental acuity. Rather, the goal is to restore the natural integration that allows your whole self to function as the unified system it actually is.

When body and mind are working together rather than against each other, energy flows more efficiently. You make better decisions because you have access to both rational analysis and intuitive wisdom. You live more completely because you stop ignoring the majority of what makes you a being. You recover more quickly from stress because your whole system is involved in the healing process.

This integration also makes hope more tangible. If you improve at reconnecting with your physical body, then hope becomes more than just an abstract concept. Hope grows into something you can feel in your body when you're connected to yourself. You get the rush of experiencing the physical sense of possibility, the embodied knowledge that you can handle whatever comes, and the felt experience of resilience, which all become available when you're present to your whole self rather than just your thinking mind.

Energy Loss and Depression

Energy depletion and depression share so many symptoms that they're often mistaken for each other. Both can cause difficulty concentrating, loss of interest in activities you used to enjoy, feelings of hopelessness, and the sense that everything requires more effort than it should. The difference lies in the underlying cause and the most effective approaches to healing.

Depression is a complex mental health condition that often requires professional support and may involve chemical imbalances that benefit from medical intervention. Energy depletion, while it can certainly contribute to depression or be worsened by it, is often more directly related to lifestyle factors and energy management practices.

When you're severely depleted, you might feel like nothing matters because you don't have the energy to connect with what does matter to you. You might feel like you can't handle basic responsibilities, not because you lack competence but because you're trying to function without adequate fuel.

The hopelessness that comes with energy depletion often lifts more quickly than clinical depression when you address the underlying energy deficit. Small changes in how you manage your energy can create noticeable improvements in mood, motivation, and outlook within days or weeks rather than months.

I am absolutely not saying that energy management is a cure for depression or that everyone who feels depressed just needs better self-care. It means that energy depletion can create or worsen mental health struggles, and addressing energy needs can be an important part of overall healing.

As mentioned earlier, Bryan was able to make some simple (not easy) changes to his lifestyle, which led to some tremendous outcomes for his energy. I needed more help with my energy depletion than a few simple tweaks that I could do on my own. I needed to meet with healthcare professionals.

There should be no shame in seeking out experts if you feel that you can't get your energy levels to where you'd like them. Start wherever you need to start. See a nutritionist, a doctor, an acupuncturist, a therapist, or any other individual who can help you find the answers. Once I met with my doctor and made a few adjustments to my life, I was able to more fully act in ways that supported my energy. At minimum, having an accountability partner can do wonders for making sure that you follow through with meeting your basic energy needs. Every reluctant gym-goer knows that it is easier to muster the motivation if there is someone relying on you to show up for them.

If you're unsure whether what you're experiencing is primarily energy depletion or something that needs professional health support, pay attention to how you respond to basic energy restoration practices. If getting adequate sleep, eating nourishing food, spending time in nature, and reducing overwhelming commitments helps significantly, energy depletion is likely a major factor.

If these practices don't help much, if you aren't sure where to start, or if you're having thoughts of self-harm, persistent feelings of worthlessness, or symptoms that interfere with your ability to function for weeks at a time, it's important to seek professional support. Energy management can complement mental health treatment, but it shouldn't replace it when clinical intervention is clearly needed to help individuals heal.

Sometimes energy depletion and depression exist together, creating a cycle where depleted energy worsens depressive symptoms, and depression makes it harder to take care of your energy needs. In these cases, working on both simultaneously with appropriate support can be more effective than addressing either one alone.

The key is to take energy depletion seriously as a real and significant factor in your overall well-being. Just because the symptoms might look like mental health issues doesn't mean they are only mental health issues. Your body and mind are connected, and caring for your energy needs is caring for your mental health.

Understanding the difference also helps you respond more effectively when you're struggling. Instead of wondering where to begin, you can ask practical questions about what your energy needs might be and how you can better meet them.

The Four Energy Types

So far, I have treated energy as a monolithic concept, one with little variance. However, energy isn't a single resource but a complex system with different energy types that interact and influence each other.[9] Understanding these different forms of energy is an excellent starting place to help aid you in identifying where your depletion is coming from and what kinds of restoration you need most.

Physical energy is the most obvious and often the first one people think of when they consider energy management. This is the fuel that powers your body through daily activities, from getting out of bed to exercising to staying alert during meetings. Physical energy comes from sleep, nutrition, movement, and taking care of your body's basic needs.

When physical energy is low, everything feels harder. Simple tasks require more effort. You might feel tired even when you haven't done anything particularly demanding. You might crave caffeine, sugar, or other quick fixes that provide temporary boosts but don't address the underlying deficit.

Restoring physical energy usually involves addressing the basics like getting adequate sleep, eating foods that nourish rather than just fill you, moving your body in ways that feel good, staying hydrated, and managing any health issues that might be draining your system.

Mental energy powers your thinking, analyzing, problem-solving, making decisions, learning new information, and staying focused on tasks that require concentration. Mental energy gets depleted by information overload, difficult decisions, complex problem-solving, and sustained concentration.

When mental energy is low, you might find yourself unable to focus on tasks that normally wouldn't be a challenge. For example, decision-making becomes overwhelming, even for simple choices. You might feel scattered or like your mind is foggy. Reading, learning, or engaging in complex conversations becomes exhausting.

Mental energy gets restored through activities that give your mind a break from intensive processing. This might include spending time in nature, engaging in mindless activities you enjoy, meditation or mindfulness practices, creative activities that don't require analysis, or simply allowing your mind to wander without forcing it to focus on anything specific.

Emotional energy is what allows you to be present with your feelings and the feelings of others. It powers empathy, emotional regulation, relationship maintenance, and your capacity to handle stress or conflict. Emotional energy gets depleted by difficult relationships, emotional labor, stress, grief, conflict, or constantly managing other people's emotions.

When emotional energy is low, you might feel numb or overwhelmed by feelings that wouldn't normally affect you so strongly. You might find yourself snapping at people you care about or withdrawing from relationships that usually bring you joy. Other people's emotions might feel like too much to handle, even when they're positive emotions.

Emotional energy gets restored through activities that help you process and release emotions. Activities that reinvigorate your emotional energy include talking with trusted friends, journaling, crying when you need to, laughing, engaging in creative expression, spending time alone to decompress, or any activity that allows your emotional system to reset.

Spiritual energy connects you to meaning, purpose, and something larger than your immediate concerns. This doesn't necessarily have anything to do with religion, though it might. Spiritual energy is what makes life feel worth living, what connects you to your values, and what gives you a sense of belonging to something meaningful.

When spiritual energy is low, life can feel pointless or empty even when everything is going well on the surface. You might feel disconnected from your values or unclear about what really matters to you. Activities that used to feel meaningful might seem hollow or unimportant.

Spiritual energy gets restored through activities that connect you to meaning such as spending time in nature, practicing gratitude, engaging in service to others, creative expression, meditation or prayer, reading or listening to material that inspires you, or any activity that reminds you of what you care about and why.

Most energy problems involve more than one type, and restoring your overall energy usually requires attention to all four areas. Someone who's physically exhausted might also be mentally exhausted from trying to keep things together, be emotionally drained from relationship stress, and be spiritually depleted from feeling disconnected from purpose. Addressing only the physical exhaustion won't fully restore their energy.

The types also influence each other. Physical depletion makes emotional regulation harder. Mental exhaustion makes it difficult to connect with spiritual meaning. Emotional overwhelm can manifest as physical fatigue.

Understanding these connections helps you create more effective restoration practices.

If you truly want to reenergize all four of these categories, then you must intentionally seek out the activities and habits in your life that support those efforts. This process is going to take some time, effort, and a lot of reflection centered around what is happening in your body and what your body is telling you. You should be asking yourself what type of energy feels depleted, what's the cause, what adjustments can I make now to invest in my energy, and what additional support will I need.

For me, what I thought was just an issue with physical energy turned out to be much deeper than that. Yes, I was indeed physically exhausted, but I had been emotionally depleted for a long time without knowing. I was carrying a lot of issues without communicating my feelings and seeking support from my loved ones. When I finally opened up to my spouse about what I was feeling, the burden was immediately lighter. It wasn't gone, just distributed a little better into my life. With that, I was able to get back to being more active by exercising regularly. These changes led to major shifts in my energy. The drains felt less draining, and I started to look at ways that I could reduce or eliminate them altogether.

Find and Protect What Energizes You

As I had just started down the path of reconnecting with myself and my energy, I came across an additional energy theory that took my understanding to the next level. Everyone has certain times, places, activities, and circumstances that naturally generate energy rather than depleting it.[10] These high energy zones are unique to each person and often go unrecognized because they feel so natural that we take them for granted. As Jim Loehr and Tony Schwartz argue in *The Power of Full Engagement*, this represents a paradigm shift in self-improvement. While countless books focus on managing time, money, or material possessions, your personal energy is what fuels everything else you do. In order to help individuals find ways to manage their energy, these scholars developed a few ways to identify energy and activities that drive them.

Identifying Your High Energy Zones

Your high energy zones are the specific conditions (times, places, activities, and people) that naturally energize rather than drain you. These zones can be categorized into several types.

Temporal High Energy Zones are certain times of day when you feel most alert and capable. For some people, this is early morning when the world is quiet and their mind is clear. For others, it's late at night when the day's obligations are finished and they can focus deeply. Some people have bursts of energy in the afternoon that they can learn to harness for important activities.

Physical High Energy Zones are spaces that help you feel more like yourself. This might be a particular room in your home, a coffee shop where you love to work, outdoor spaces that restore your spirit, or environments that support the kind of energy you want to cultivate.

Activity-Based High Energy Zones include tasks or pursuits that leave you feeling more energized after doing them than you felt before. They might include certain types of exercise, creative projects, learning about topics that fascinate you, or any activity that feeds your soul while you're doing it.

Relational High Energy Zones are individuals who bring out your best self, who energize you through their presence, who make you feel more capable and optimistic after spending time with them. They might be friends who share your values, colleagues who inspire you, or family members who accept you completely.

The Energy Quadrants Framework

Loehr and Schwartz explain that to effectively manage your energy across these zones, we need to understand how each activity we choose to engage in impacts our overall energy levels. To facilitate these decisions, Loehr and Schwartz provide a crucial framework through their Energy Quadrants model (See Fig. 1).

Each quadrant of the figure represents a combination of energy quality vs energy required to complete. The vertical axis moves from high energy required at the top to low energy required at the bottom. The horizontal axis moves from negative energy activities to positive energy activities on the right. Combining the two creates four quadrants. Understanding how each quadrant functions is one of the key objectives to master in order to fully build your Energy Pillar of Hope.

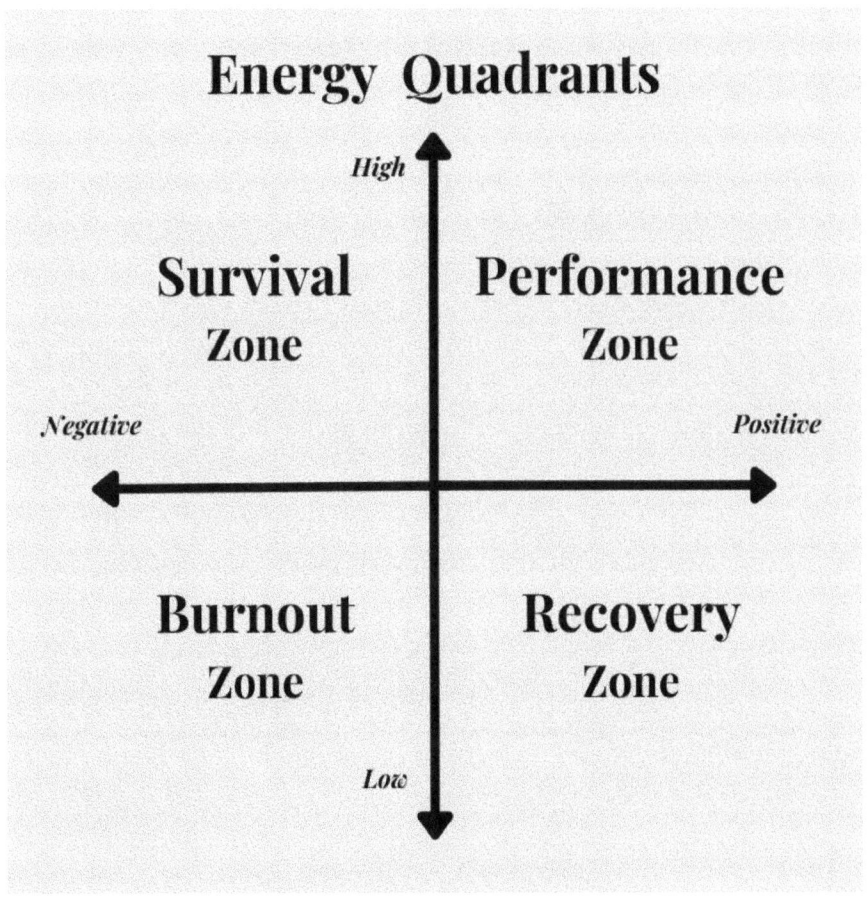

(Figure 1: The Energy Quadrants)

High Positive Quadrant (Performance) contains activities that add positive energy to your life and require high levels of energy. These include passion projects that require your full engagement, focus, and effort to complete. This quadrant contains your most important work done during your peak energy times.

Low Positive Quadrant (Recovery) consists of behaviors that require little energy to complete while adding positive energy to your life. These are recovery activities that "sharpen the saw" such as meditation, gentle walks, reading for pleasure, or spending quiet time in energizing spaces.

High Negative Quadrant (Survival) includes activities that drain energy while requiring high engagement. This sector includes crisis management, difficult confrontations, or working during your naturally low-energy times.

Low Negative Quadrant (Burnout) encompasses low-energy activities that also drain you. We all recognize this area by mindless scrolling, toxic relationships, or environments that consistently deplete rather than restore.

The Critical 80/20 Ratio

The key finding from Loehr and Schwartz is that the most driven, highly-motivated, and energized individuals don't spend 100% of their time in the Performance Zone. Instead, they recognize the rhythm of effort and recovery. They recommend an 80/20 split: for every hour you spend in the upper quadrants (high energy activities), you need 10-20 minutes engaged in Recovery Zone activities.

This ratio prevents burnout and ensures sustainable high performance. Without adequate time in the Recovery Zone quadrant, you'll inevitably crash into the Burnout Zone.

Protecting and Leveraging Your High Energy Zones

Once you've identified your high energy zones and understand the quadrant framework, the next step is strategic protection and utilization:

Schedule strategically by placing your most important activities during your high-energy times when possible. This means protecting these temporal zones from Low Negative activities.

Create supportive environments by spending time in spaces that naturally energize you or by modifying existing spaces to better support your energy.

Prioritize energizing activities by building more Low Positive and High Positive activities into your routine while minimizing time spent in negative quadrants.

Cultivate energizing relationships by spending more time with people who bring out your best self while setting boundaries with those who consistently drain your energy.

You shouldn't be trying to avoid challenging activities or looking for ways to spend all your time in the Performance Zone. It's about being strategic with your energy so you have enough fuel for what matters most. When you're operating from your high energy zones and managing your energy quadrants effectively, you have more capacity to handle difficult situations and more to give to others.

Expanding Your Energy Zones

Some high energy zones can be cultivated or expanded. If you notice that a particular environment energizes you, you might be able to create similar conditions in other spaces. If certain Recovery Zone activities restore your energy better than others, you can build more of them into your routine.

Other high energy zones need to be protected as they are. If you have limited time with energizing people, that time becomes precious and worth guarding. If you have only certain hours when your energy peaks, those hours deserve priority for your most important work.

The ultimate goal with managing your energy is to recognize and protect these sources of natural energy while strategically managing your movement through all four energy quadrants so they can sustain you through the parts of life that are more challenging or draining.

Approaches for Energy Drains

Obviously, not all energy drains can be eliminated from your life. Some are temporary and necessary parts of growth or change. Others are ongoing realities that come with responsibilities you've chosen or circumstances you can't control. Learning to work with unavoidable energy drains through personal practices can make them more manageable.

In order to really get the most of your focus on energy, you must seek and develop activities, exercises, or strategies that help you recover from energy depletion or prevent it from accumulating to overwhelming levels. Unlike generic advice about self-care, these personal approaches are tailored specifically to your needs, preferences, and circumstances.

What works as a rejuvenating practice for one person might be completely ineffective or even draining for another. Some people restore energy through social connection, while others need solitude. Some find physical activity reinvigorating, while others need complete rest. Some benefit from structured activities, while others need unstructured time.

The key is discovering what actually works for you rather than what you think should work or what works for other people. This requires experimentation and honest self-assessment about what leaves you feeling better versus what just fills time or numbs difficult feelings.

Effective personal approaches usually address the specific type of energy depletion you're experiencing. If you're mentally exhausted from decision-making and problem-solving, you need activities that give your analytical mind a rest. If you're emotionally drained from relationship stress, you need practices that help you process and release emotions.

Some therapeutic practices work **preventively**, helping you maintain energy reserves before they become completely depleted. These might include regular practices that keep your energy flowing. You could include activities such as daily walks, weekly phone calls with supportive friends, monthly creative projects, or seasonal retreats that provide an escape from overstimulating environments.

Other practices work **restoratively**, helping you recover after periods of high energy expenditure. These are the activities you turn to when you're already depleted and need to rebuild your reserves. They might include longer periods of rest, intensive self-care practices, temporary withdrawal from demanding activities, or seeking additional support.

Time-based strategies involve managing how you spend your time to protect and restore energy. This might include creating buffer time between demanding activities, scheduling restoration activities as seriously as you schedule obligations, or building in recovery time after you know you'll be dealing with energy drains.

Environment-based activities involve creating or seeking out physical spaces that support your energy. This might mean decluttering spaces that feel chaotic, adding elements that bring you peace, spending time in nature, or temporary changes to your environment when you're feeling depleted.

Social supports involve managing your social energy through conscious choices about relationships and interactions. This might include spending more time with energizing people when you're depleted, taking breaks from demanding relationships when possible, or seeking out social support that meets your specific needs.

Activity-based practices involve choosing to participate in those things that restore rather than drain your energy. The key is being honest about what actually helps versus what you feel like you should do. If exercise energizes you, it's therapeutic. If it exhausts you when you're already depleted, it's not. Maybe it's the type of exercise or the intensity, but you can look for ways to make it energizing instead of depleting.

Finally, **creative expression** can be particularly beneficial because it allows energy to move and transform rather than just being consumed. This might include writing, art, music, crafting, gardening, cooking, or any activity that allows you to create something rather than just consume or maintain.

For me, one rejuvenating practice that would restore my energy was daily morning exercise. If I wait until my energy is depleted later in the day, I can never muster up the willpower to do any sort of physical exercise. I have to do it as part of my morning routine. Likewise, if I skip a morning (or two), those days usually end up feeling like a grind. My thoughts are muddled, and I am way less productive than if I just get moving in the morning.

Figure out what works for you because the most important aspect of finding your personal list of energizing activities is consistency and self-compassion. These practices work best when they're integrated into your life regularly rather than saved for crisis moments. They also work better when you approach them with kindness toward yourself rather than as another obligation to perform perfectly. With that, you will need to understand the next Pillar to make these practices a natural part of your routines.

Stone Upon Stone—Building Your Pillar

Base

Energy Assessment:

Complete this comprehensive energy assessment to understand your current energy patterns. For each statement, rate yourself on a scale of 1-5 (1 = never true, 5 = always true):

Physical Energy:
1. I wake up feeling rested most mornings
2. I have consistent energy throughout my day without major crashes
3. I listen to my body's signals for hunger, thirst, and rest
4. I engage in movement that feels energizing rather than depleting

Mental Energy:
5. I can focus on complex tasks without feeling mentally exhausted quickly

6. I take breaks before my concentration completely depletes

7. I protect time for mental rest and restoration

8. I notice when information overload is affecting my thinking

Emotional Energy:

9. I can be present with others' emotions without feeling drained

10. I process my own emotions rather than pushing through them

11. I maintain healthy boundaries in emotionally demanding relationships

12. I seek support when carrying emotional burdens

Spiritual Energy:

13. I feel connected to activities and values that give my life meaning

14. I experience moments of awe, gratitude, or transcendence regularly

15. I have practices that connect me to something larger than myself

16. My daily activities align with what I find personally meaningful

Reflection Questions:

- Which energy type scored lowest for you? What specific situations or relationships consistently drain this type of energy?

- Think of a recent day when you felt energized and engaged. Map out that day hour by hour - what patterns do you notice in terms of timing, activities, people, and environments?

- Complete this sentence: "I know I'm running on empty when I start to _____."

- Identify your current "just tired" patterns. What are you really experiencing beneath that phrase? Is it physical exhaustion, mental fog, emotional overwhelm, or spiritual emptiness?

Body-Mind Connection Check:

Spend 5 minutes doing a body scan from head to toe. Notice:

- Where do you hold tension?

- What does your breathing pattern tell you about your current state?

- Are there physical sensations you've been ignoring?

° How connected do you feel to your physical self right now?

Pay attention to what your body is telling you about your energy levels.

Column

The Energy Quadrants Challenge:

For the next seven days, you'll track your energy using Loehr and Schwartz's Energy Quadrants framework while implementing specific energy management practices:

Days 1-2: Energy Tracking

Create a simple log tracking your noticeable activities for 48 hours using these categories:
- ° High Positive (Performance): Activities that energize you and require high engagement
- ° Low Positive (Recovery): Low-energy activities that restore you
- ° High Negative (Survival): High-energy activities that drain you
- ° Low Negative (Burnout): Low-energy activities that also deplete you

For each activity, note:
- ° Which quadrant it falls into
- ° Your energy level before (1-10) and after (1-10)
- ° The time of day
- ° Your physical location and who you were with

Days 3-4: Intentional Energy Allocation

Based on your tracking, implement these changes:
- ° Schedule one important task during your identified high-energy time
- ° Add 15-20 minutes of Recovery Zone activities after every hour of high-energy work
- ° Identify one Low Negative activity you can eliminate or minimize
- ° Choose one body-mind reconnection practice from the chapter (conscious breathing, tension release, mindful movement, etc.) and use it three times daily

Days 5-7: Energy Protection Practice

Focus on protecting and expanding your energy zones:
- ° Identify your top 2 energy-draining situations from your tracking
- ° Implement one specific boundary or modification for each drain
- ° Schedule one energizing activity daily during your natural high-energy time
- ° Practice saying "no" to one Low Negative activity that requests your time
- ° Spend 10 minutes daily in an environment that naturally energizes you

Daily Documentation:

Each evening, write brief responses to:

- What did I learn about my energy patterns today?
- When did I feel most integrated (body and mind working together)?
- How did protecting my energy affect my interactions with others?
- What resistance did I notice when trying to honor my energy needs?

End-of-Week Integration:

- Which energy quadrant do you spend the most time in?
- How might you shift this balance?
- What specific changes will you make to better protect your high-energy zones?
- How can you build more Recovery Zone activities into your regular routine?
- What support (medical, professional, or personal) might you need to address deeper energy issues?

Capstone

Books:

The Power of Full Engagement by Jim Loehr and Tony Schwartz

Burnout: The Secret to Unlocking the Stress Cycle by Nagoski and Nagoski

The Body Keeps the Score by Bessel van der Kolk

Rest is Resistance by Tricia Hersey

Podcasts:

The Energy Management Podcast with Michelle Segar

Feel Better, Live More with Dr Rangan Chatterjee

On Being: "The Wisdom of Your Body"

The Happiness Lab: "The Science of Well-Being and Energy"

Articles:

"Managing Your Energy, Not Your Time" (Harvard Business Review)

"The Science of Energy Management" (Journal of Occupational Health Psychology)

"Physical Activity and Energy Levels" (American Psychological Association)

"The Connection Between Sleep and Mental Energy" (Sleep Foundation)

Chapter Notes:

1. **Mental hyperactivity and energy depletion:** Research in cognitive psychology demonstrates that rumination and overthinking create measurable physiological stress responses, including elevated cortisol levels and increased metabolic demands. Studies show that mental hyperactivity can be as energetically costly as physical exertion, particularly when the thinking patterns are repetitive or anxiety-based.

2. **Sleep apnea prevalence and diagnosis:** The American Academy of Sleep Medicine reports that sleep apnea affects approximately 26% of adults between 30-70 years old, with many cases remaining undiagnosed. Research indicates that untreated sleep apnea can reduce energy levels by 40-60% and significantly impact hormone regulation, even in individuals without obvious risk factors.

3. **Energy deficit compounding effects:** Studies in occupational psychology show that energy depletion creates a cascading effect where each day's unrestored energy debt makes the following day's demands feel more overwhelming. This compound effect explains why small energy management improvements can create disproportionately large improvements in overall functioning.

4. **Rest as requirement vs. reward research:** Neuroscientific studies demonstrate that the brain's default mode network requires regular downtime to process information and restore cognitive resources. Research from Harvard Medical School shows that cultures promoting "earned rest" create higher rates of burnout and decreased creativity compared to those treating rest as essential for optimal performance.

5. **Mind-body separation in modern life:** Research in embodied cognition shows that the artificial separation between mental and physical experience contradicts how the brain actually processes information. Studies indicate that people who maintain stronger mind-body connections show better emotional regulation, decision-making abilities, and stress resilience.

6. **Sleep ritual effectiveness:** Clinical sleep research demonstrates that consistent pre-sleep rituals improve sleep quality by 23-30% by helping regulate circadian rhythms and reducing cortisol levels. The National Sleep Foundation's research shows that treating sleep as sacred rather than optional correlates with better energy levels and immune function.

7. **Nature connection and restoration:** Environmental psychology research shows that even brief nature exposure (5-10 minutes) can reduce cortisol levels, lower blood pressure, and improve mood. Studies from the University of Michigan demonstrate that nature connection helps restore directed attention capacity and reduces mental fatigue more effectively than urban environments.

8. **Depression vs. energy depletion differentiation:** Clinical research in psychiatry shows that while depression and chronic fatigue share 70% of symptoms, they respond differently to interventions. Studies indicate that energy-focused interventions show rapid improvement (days to weeks) when energy depletion is primary, while clinical depression typically requires longer-term treatment approaches.

9. **Multi-dimensional energy systems:** Research from the Institute of HeartMath and other energy psychology organizations demonstrates that human energy operates through interconnected physical, mental, emotional, and spiritual systems. Studies in areas such as positive psychology and integrative health indicate that interventions addressing multiple aspects of well-being tend to be more effective than single-focus approaches.

10. **Loehr and Schwartz energy management research:** Published research from the Human Performance Institute helped develop the energy-based performance approaches as alternatives to traditional management strategies. Their framework has been applied in corporate and athletic settings, and the general principles align with research in psychology and human performance showing that energy management can be more effective than time management for sustainable performance.

5: H - Habits
Building the Skills for Hope

One year, I had a little bit of a line forming at Parent Teacher Conferences. I met each parent, went over their student's work, and sent them on to the next teacher. I had just finished going through the standard PTC routine with a student and her parents when the next mom sat down in the seat in front of me. I started out the routine by asking who her student was. She explained that she didn't have a student who was currently in my class, but her son was in my class the year prior.

I didn't usually have visits with parents of kids not in my class, so I was thrown off a bit and asked how I could help. She asked if I remembered a pep talk that I gave my students the year before. I told her that I give a lot of pep talks, so I didn't really know what she was referring to.

She explained that her son had always struggled as a student. He wasn't failing out of his classes, but he sort of glided through school by doing the bare minimum, which was hurting his GPA. He never liked school and didn't see the point until about halfway through his sophomore year of high school, the year he had my class. He finished the second semester of his sophomore year with excellent grades, and, she added, this junior year he was keeping what he started, doing even better than he ever had.

She could tell that I was still confused because I had no clue what this had to do with me. She finished the conversation by telling me how thankful she was that her son had me as a teacher because she had recently asked her son what changed. He told her, "It was a speech that Mr. Drake had given in my class. Mr. Drake taught us that the formula for being successful in school is simple: show up on time, at least act like you're paying attention, and turn everything back to the teacher when it's due. Master those three things, and you almost can't help but be successful at school."

I gave her a heartfelt thank you because most parents don't take the time to share such things. Then, she left, and I sat there thinking about how this simple pep talk that I give to every class a couple times a year impacted this student so much. Honestly, I thought that most of those discussions fell flat based on how many students continued to turn their assignments in late, but I knew that I had to do something to try and emphasize the importance that building good habits would have on these students if they were willing to take advantage of my insights.

My fascination with the power of simple habits didn't begin in that classroom, though. It started years earlier during my undergraduate studies. At the start of every semester, the first day of class was always my most anxiety-riddled experience of the course. I don't get test anxiety, and I'm pretty good at getting through papers and assignments in a crunch. However, after attending all of my courses the first day and receiving the syllabus for each course, I would always experience a moment of nerve-inducing panic that verged on total breakdown. Why? Because seeing the entirety of each course laid in front of me (with each assignment, paper, reading, and exam) caused a complete overload.

How was I going to manage all that needed to be done? It always seemed like an ungodly amount of effort was going to be required. Now, I made it through intact, but it was in those days when I really started to understand the power that habits have to shape the outcomes of our lives. If you can build the habits, you give yourself an exponentially greater possibility for the life you seek. This understanding became part of the message I shared with my students about showing up on time, paying attention, and turning stuff in. These weren't just school strategies. They were the habits that would be most beneficial for them to focus on in any area of life.

Since then, I have worked with many individuals to put new habits into place, and the pattern remains consistent. The most transformative changes really do come from simple, repeated actions that compound over time.[1]

Different professions might call habits different names. In education, we are trained to implement routines and procedures to help the classroom environment. Similarly, a hospital might have specific checklists that must be implemented as part of every regimen. Journeymen might follow guidelines established in building codes that require specific approaches to construction. Each of these examples highlights the importance of routine habits in our professional lives. If habits are so important to our professions, then they must be equally important to our personal lives as well. Whether you approach your habits as a routine, a checklist, or some other methodology, developing systems that make personal improvement automatic is one of the only paths towards better outcomes in our lives.

In the WE HOPE model, Habit is where action begins to happen and where hope takes root in our daily lives. Worth and Energy are important pillars of the framework, but the primary ways we act to influence them are through our habits. Without properly implemented habits, the other aspects of the WE HOPE model crumble into the despair-filled world of disappointment and unfulfillment. Throughout this chapter, you will acquire some critical tools in your arsenal to shape the habits that you deem necessary in your path towards more hopeful learning and living.

Understanding Motivation

When people talk about creating lasting change, they almost always start with motivation. They assume that if you just want something badly enough, if you can just find the right inspiration, or if you create enough urgency, you'll naturally do what needs to be done. This approach feels logical, but it misses something crucial about how human behavior actually works.

Motivation is not a reliable foundation for change. It comes and goes like weather, influenced by your mood, your energy levels, your circumstances, and a dozen other factors you can't control.[2] The person who feels incredibly motivated on Sunday night to start exercising might feel completely different on

Tuesday morning when the alarm goes off. The motivation that felt so powerful in that moment has evaporated, leaving behind only the hard reality of having to do something difficult.

Motivation is also highly personal. What motivates one person might have no effect on another, or might even be demotivating. Some people are motivated by competition, while others are motivated by collaboration. Some are energized by big, ambitious goals, while others prefer small, concrete steps. Some respond to external rewards, while others are driven by internal satisfaction.

Additionally, past experiences shape what motivates you in ways you might not even realize. If you've been praised for being helpful, you might be motivated by opportunities to serve others. If you've been criticized for not being disciplined enough, you might be motivated by proving you can stick to something. If you've experienced failure in the past, you might be motivated by the desire to avoid that feeling again, or you might be motivated by the chance to finally succeed.

When you lack motivation, it doesn't mean you have a major flaw in your character. Motivation was never designed to sustain long-term behavior change.[3] It's meant to get you started, to provide the initial spark that moves you from thinking about change to taking the first step, but after that initial push, something else needs to take over if the change is going to last.

What takes over is habit. Habits are behaviors that have become automatic through repetition. They don't require motivation because they're not really decisions anymore. They're just what you do. You don't need to motivate yourself to brush your teeth in the morning or check your email when you're at work. These actions happen automatically because they've been repeated so many times that they've become part of your routine.

The challenge is that motivation feels more exciting than habits. Motivation promises dramatic transformation, immediate results, and the thrill of finally becoming the person you've always wanted to be with little effort and no price to pay. Habits promise something much less glamorous but infinitely more valuable. They promise that change can happen, that the behaviors that seemed impossible when you were relying on motivation can become as natural as breathing.

Understanding that motivation is temporary doesn't mean you should ignore it completely. Motivation can be incredibly useful for getting started and for pushing through particularly difficult moments. The key is recognizing its limitations and building systems that don't depend on it.

One of my favorite theories of motivation is the Valence x (times) Expectancy model.[4] The model treats motivation like a math equation. Valence refers to how much you value the outcome you're working toward. Expectancy refers to how much you believe you can actually achieve that outcome. Multiply the two together, and you end up with your level of motivation for said activity. If either number is zero, then the motivation level is zero. Motivation is highest when both value and expectation are high, when you really want something and you believe you can get it.

This formula helps uncover why the same goal can be incredibly motivating for one person and completely uninspiring for another. It also explains why your motivation for the same goal can change depending on your circumstances. When you're feeling confident and capable, your expectancy is high, so your motivation increases. When you're feeling overwhelmed or defeated, your expectancy drops, and your motivation disappears even if you still want the outcome just as much.

Thus, before you begin starting a new habit, ask yourself how much you value the outcome. Is the effort going to be worth the sacrifice? Next, you have to be completely and utterly honest with yourself as you ask if you have the confidence that you will be successful. If the number is high on both, you have much better odds for success in the end. If you're unsure, you might need to cycle back to the Pillars of Energy and Worth. Now that you have some key understandings about motivation, you may be able to be more intentional with how you read and implement those Pillars.

Your Comfort Zone Limits You

Habits are usually established to keep us within our comfort zone. Your comfort zone isn't just a metaphor. It's a real psychological space where your brain feels safe and doesn't have to work very hard. Within your comfort zone, you know what to expect, you know how to respond, and you can operate on autopilot without much stress or uncertainty. This zone serves an important function by conserving mental energy and reducing anxiety, but it also creates invisible barriers that can keep you stuck in patterns that no longer serve you.

The comfort zone becomes limiting when it shrinks to the point where it excludes the very experiences you need for growth, healing, or positive change. When you've been hurt, disappointed, or overwhelmed, it's natural for your comfort zone to contract as a protective mechanism. You avoid situations that feel risky, relationships that might lead to vulnerability, or activities that might result in failure. This protection helps you feel safe in the short term, but it can also cut you off from opportunities for hope and renewal.

The paradox of the comfort zone is that it often becomes uncomfortable over time. What starts as a safe haven can gradually become a prison. You might find yourself feeling restless, bored, or vaguely dissatisfied even though you're not doing anything particularly challenging or risky. This discomfort is often a signal that your comfort zone has become too small for who you're becoming or who you want to be.

Expanding your comfort zone doesn't require dramatic leaps or reckless risks. Small, consistent steps outside your current boundaries can gradually increase your capacity for uncertainty and challenge. Each time you do something slightly outside your comfort zone and survive the experience, your brain updates its definition of what's safe. What felt scary or impossible yesterday can become routine tomorrow through repeated exposure.

The key is designing new habits that expand your comfort zone and increase your possibilities. To accomplish this, we must first distinguish between productive discomfort and unnecessary suffering. Productive discomfort is the feeling you get when you're stretching yourself in service of something you care about. It might feel scary, but it should also feel meaningful. You're growing, learning, or moving toward something important to you. Unnecessary suffering, on the other hand, is pain without purpose, stress without benefit, or risk without reasonable hope of reward.

Your comfort zone around hope, specifically, might be smaller than you realize. If you've experienced significant disappointments, you might have unconsciously decided that hoping for anything good is too risky. You protect yourself from future disappointment by not allowing yourself to want things too much or believe that positive change is possible. This creates a different kind of suffering, which is the slow ache of living without hope.

Expanding your comfort zone around hope means gradually allowing yourself to want things again, to believe that good things are possible, and to take small actions based on that belief even when you can't guarantee the outcome. This expansion happens through practice.

The process of expanding your comfort zone is itself a habit that can be developed. The more you practice tolerating uncertainty and discomfort in service of your values and purpose, the easier it becomes. Your capacity for growth expands like a muscle that gets stronger with use.

For me, the process of writing this book is an effort to get out of the habits that have made me comfortable. I could be perfectly happy not putting my ideas out there. The arena is a scary place, and I get criticized by outsiders enough in my day-to-day job that I don't particularly love the idea of other people reading this work and tearing it to shreds. I created and cared for these ideas. I have spent countless hours researching and developing them. Putting these Pillars out to the world is a little unnerving. My comfort zone is to keep my ideas and opinions private. Hold on to them and care for them in a space where no one else can criticize. However, if I kept them hidden, not only am I limiting my growth, I would be keeping what I find valuable and important hidden from the world, and I wouldn't be abiding by my own philosophy.

Recognizing the boundaries of your current comfort zone is the first step toward expanding it. Notice what you avoid, what you tell yourself you "can't" do, or what makes you feel anxious just thinking about it. Some of these boundaries might be serving you well and should be respected. Others might be outdated protective mechanisms that are now holding you back from the life you desperately want to live.

You absolutely need to keep safe spaces where you can rest, recharge, and operate with confidence. You don't want to eliminate your comfort zone entirely. The goal is to ensure that your comfort zone is large enough to include the new habits where you can build experiences, relationships, and activities that are essential for your well-being and growth. Your new habits should be those small incremental changes that permit the comfort zone to creep continually larger until you look back at the old you and realize how much you've grown.

The Science: Small Wins

Most people don't struggle to set goals. They struggle to build systems that are small enough to maintain and meaningful enough to matter. We think change needs to feel dramatic, but real transformation often starts with some very simple habits of hope.

If you desire to expand your comfort zone and build new and lasting habits, you have to learn to hack the process. For this sort of habit hacking, there are few books as good as James Clear's *Atomic Habits*.[5] Many resources on habit exist, but this book's premise and practical advice make a truly inspired work. I'm providing a brief overview of the main concepts, but to really apply the Pillar of Habit, you will need to deep dive on the topic and spend some time delving into this book and others.

To begin, Clear recognizes that the human brain is wired to respond powerfully to success, even small success. When you accomplish something, even something minor, your brain releases dopamine, which not only makes you feel good but also reinforces the behavior that led to that success.[6] This neurochemical reward system is what makes small wins so effective for creating lasting change.

Small wins, according to Clear, work because they create positive momentum without overwhelming your system. When you set enormous goals that require dramatic changes, you're fighting against your brain's natural resistance to change. Your brain perceives big changes as threats and activates stress responses that make it harder to think clearly, make good decisions, or maintain consistent behavior.

Small wins sidestep this resistance by flying under your brain's threat-detection radar. A five-minute walk doesn't feel threatening. Writing one sentence doesn't trigger overwhelm. Making your bed doesn't require heroic motivation. These tiny actions feel manageable, so your brain doesn't fight against them. When you successfully complete these small actions, you get the neurochemical reward without the stress.

Consider these concepts in light of the Expectancy x Valence Model. The compound effect of small wins is what creates lasting transformation. Each small success builds confidence and an expectation that you will continue winning as you progress through building your new habit.

Research on habit formation shows that the brain creates neural pathways through repetition. Each time you perform a behavior, you strengthen the neural pathway associated with that behavior. Small, consistent actions create stronger neural pathways than large, inconsistent ones because consistency is what builds the automatic response that defines a habit.

The key insight from neuroscience is that your brain changes based on what you repeatedly do, not based on what you occasionally do with great intensity. A person who writes for ten minutes every day will develop stronger writing habits and skills than someone who writes occasionally for extended periods of time. Even though the occasional writer might spend more total time writing, the consistent writer benefits from the regular habit.

Small wins also help you gather evidence that change is possible. When you're struggling with hopelessness, your brain has likely collected substantial evidence that change is difficult or impossible. Small wins provide counter-evidence. They prove to your skeptical mind that you are capable of following through on commitments, that positive change is possible, and that you have more control over your life than you might have believed.

The psychological impact of small wins extends beyond the specific behavior you're changing. Success in one small area tends to increase confidence and motivation in other areas of life.[7] This spillover effect means that developing one small habit can catalyze improvements across multiple domains of your life.

Habits are easy to associate with our physical well-being, so fitness and health tend to be overutilized as examples of how to apply habits. Don't assume that this is the only area where you will find the Pillar of Habits to be useful.

For example, once I understood the science of small wins, I successfully used the systems to "trick" my high school students to develop better writing habits. Early on in my career, I would hand out the requirements for an essay and turn the students loose to finish. The typical student would either give up, submit something plagiarized, or never get started in the first place.

Then, I made a shift where I sought small wins along the way. At the beginning of each writing unit, I made the first assignments so easy that it was nearly impossible for a student to fail. I would start with such a simple prompt. *Write one sentence answering the question on the board.* The next day, I would ask them to come up with a few reasons why they took the stance they did the day before. We would continue with a variety of prompts and discussions. Each small victory led up to the unveiling of the essay assignment. The big reveal was that they had already completed over half the assignment before they knew they were even working on it. After so many small wins, they couldn't help but recognize that they had developed the habits to be successful on the final draft.

The essay assignment design and the science behind my shift in curriculum approaches reveal that "going big" often backfires. When you attempt dramatic changes, you're more likely to experience setbacks and failures. These failures don't just prevent progress. They actively undermine your confidence and reinforce beliefs about your inability to change. Each failure becomes evidence that supports hopelessness rather than hope.

Small wins create the opposite dynamic. Even when you have setbacks, they feel less significant in the context of multiple small successes. You develop resilience and self-compassion because you have evidence of your capability, making it easier to get back on track after temporary lapses.

The timing of small wins matters too. Getting early wins in any change process is crucial for maintaining motivation and building momentum. This is why effective habit formation focuses on making the initial behavior so small and easy that success is almost guaranteed.

Designing Habits That Stick

Creating habits that actually last requires understanding how habits work in your brain and designing them to work with your psychology rather than against it. Most people approach habit formation backwards, starting with what they think they should do rather than what they're actually capable of sustaining.

Going back to Clear's work, the basic structure of any habit involves four components that researchers call the habit loop. The **cue** triggers a **craving**. Our **cravings** lead to a **response** which is followed by a **reward**. The **response** is the behavior itself, and the **reward** reinforces the behavior and makes it more likely to happen again. Understanding these components allows you to design habits intentionally rather than hoping they'll develop naturally.

The cue is what tells your brain to initiate the habit. Effective cues are specific, obvious, and already part of your existing routine. Instead of relying on time-based cues like "I'll exercise at 6 AM," which require you to remember and check the time, you can use event-based cues like "After I pour my first cup of coffee, I'll do ten pushups." The coffee-pouring is something you already do automatically, so it becomes a reliable trigger for the new behavior.

Environmental cues are often more effective than mental reminders because they don't rely on your memory or willpower. Leaving your workout clothes visible reminds you to exercise. Placing a book on your pillow reminds you to read before bed. Putting healthy snacks at eye level in your refrigerator makes nutritious choices more automatic.

The response should be the smallest version of the behavior that still feels meaningful to you. If you want to develop a reading habit, start with reading one page per day rather than committing to reading for an hour. If you want to exercise regularly, begin with a five-minute walk rather than a full workout. The goal is to make the behavior so easy that you can do it even on your worst days.

Starting small doesn't mean that your habits will stay small forever. It's about building the neural pathway and the identity of someone who does this behavior consistently. Once the habit is established, you can gradually increase the intensity, duration, or complexity. However, premature expansion is one of the most common reasons habits fail.

Clear further explains that the reward component is what makes your brain want to repeat the behavior. Some behaviors have natural rewards built in. Exercise releases endorphins that make you feel good. Creative activities provide the satisfaction of making something. Social connections offer emotional fulfillment. Other behaviors might need artificial rewards, especially in the beginning when the natural benefits aren't yet apparent.

Effective rewards are immediate, satisfying, and aligned with the identity you're trying to build. If you're trying to become someone who prioritizes health, rewarding yourself with unhealthy food after exercise sends mixed messages to your brain. Better rewards might include checking off a habit tracker, taking a relaxing shower, or spending a few minutes doing something you enjoy.

Habit stacking is a powerful technique that involves attaching new habits to existing ones.[8] Since your current habits are already automatic, they make reliable cues for new behaviors. The formula is simple: "After (current habit), I will (new habit)." This approach leverages the neural pathways you've already built rather than trying to create entirely new ones.

Environmental design plays a crucial role in habit formation. Your environment should make good habits easier and bad habits harder. This might mean preparing healthy meals in advance so good nutrition doesn't require decision-making when you're tired and hungry. It might mean removing distracting apps from your phone so focused work becomes more natural. Your physical context makes forming a habit much easier if you are consistent with your space. Reading is much easier to complete if you find yourself at your favorite reading location regularly.

In addition to knowing the physical environment, timing is an important concept to consider. The two-day rule is a simple but effective principle for maintaining habits when life gets complicated. The rule states that you never allow yourself to go more than two days without performing your habit. This gives you flexibility for the realities of life while preventing the complete breakdown that often happens when people adopt an all-or-nothing mentality.

Finally, identity reinforcement is perhaps the most powerful aspect of habit formation.[1] Every time you perform a habit, you're casting a vote for the type of person you want to become. Each small action is evidence that supports a new identity. As with my essay writing students, I had to change their identities from "students who dreaded writing" to an identity of "students who might not like writing but could tolerate the process." My big dream was to help them form an identity of "writers," but they were still high school students, and I was not always a miracle worker.

Based on these concepts, here are two tips for developing a system for building the Pillar of Habits in your own life. First, be specific in designing your new habit. In order to identify the specifics of a habit, I prefer to put the steps of the routine in a checklist format. For example, just like most millennials these days, I have started to be drawn to gardening in my backyard. At first, I had no idea what I should be doing at different times to organize, maintain, and harvest a small garden. Each phase of gardening has a certain routine and rhythm to it. As I've learned and applied different practices, I've formulated some daily, weekly, and seasonal checklists that help ensure that I don't skip any steps. You can take a lot of the work out of these checklists by having AI give you a starting point. Then, you can customize them to your needs.

The second insight is to automate your habit triggers. Again, technology comes into play with my automations. I have a few different digital calendars that I use to accomplish this. The garden example comes to mind here. I have a calendar set up that reminds me when to water, when to prune, when to fertilize, and when to take care of pests and weeds. With the help of AI, it took just a few hours to set up and fine tune. Combining the checklist approach with digital reminders is my system, but you should develop a habit-building system that works for you.

Building Habits That Support Hope

Hope isn't just a feeling that happens to you. It's a capacity that can be developed through specific practices and habits. Just as you can build physical strength through consistent exercise, you can build your capacity for hope through consistent behaviors that reinforce the three components of hope: having goals, finding pathways, and developing agency.

Goal-setting habits help you maintain clear direction even when you're feeling lost or overwhelmed. This doesn't mean creating elaborate life plans or setting unrealistic expectations. It means developing regular practices that help you clarify what matters to you and what you want to move toward. Weekly reflection sessions, monthly check-ins with your values, or daily practices of setting small intentions all build your capacity to maintain direction.

The habit of writing down three things you want to accomplish each day, no matter how small, trains your brain to think in terms of possibility and forward movement. Even on difficult days, this practice helps you identify tiny steps you can take rather than feeling completely paralyzed by circumstances.

Pathway-thinking habits involve regularly practicing the mental skill of finding multiple routes to your goals. This might involve brainstorming sessions where you deliberately generate different approaches to challenges you're facing.

It might mean seeking out stories of people who've overcome similar obstacles. It might involve learning new skills that expand your options for addressing problems.

The habit of asking "What else could I try?" when you encounter obstacles builds mental flexibility and reduces the hopelessness that comes from feeling like you only have one option. Even when the alternatives aren't immediately practical, the mental exercise of generating possibilities keeps your brain oriented toward solutions rather than stuck in problems.

Agency-building habits focus on strengthening your sense of personal power and effectiveness. These are behaviors that remind you that you have influence over your life, even when that influence feels limited. Daily practices that involve making choices, taking action, or exercising control in small ways all contribute to your sense of agency.

Physical movement is one of the most powerful agency-building habits because it directly connects intention with action.[15] When you move your body intentionally, you experience visceral proof that you can translate thoughts into reality. This doesn't require intense exercise. Even gentle stretching or short walks reinforce the connection between what you decide to do and what actually happens.

Habits that involve creating something rather than just consuming also build agency. Writing, drawing, cooking, gardening, crafting, or any activity where you transform raw materials into something new provides tangible evidence of your ability to influence the world around you.

Habits that emphasize learning new skills support hope by expanding your sense of what's possible. When you regularly expose yourself to new information, skills, or perspectives, you stretch your understanding of what options exist. This might involve reading books, listening to podcasts, taking classes, or having conversations with people who have different experiences than you do.

Connection habits involve regular practices that maintain and strengthen your relationships with other people.[16] Hope is often easier to maintain when you don't feel alone in your struggles. This might mean scheduling regular phone calls with friends, participating in communities that share your interests or values, or simply making small gestures that maintain your social bonds.

The habit of expressing gratitude regularly helps rewire your brain to notice positive aspects of your life that might otherwise go unrecognized.[17] This doesn't mean pretending everything is fine or minimizing real problems. It means training your attention to include good things along with difficulties, creating a more balanced and realistic perspective.

Service habits, even very small ones, connect you to purposes larger than your immediate concerns. This might involve volunteering, helping neighbors, mentoring someone, or any regular practice that allows you to contribute to others' well-being. These habits remind you that you matter and that your actions can make a positive difference.

The key to building hope-supporting habits is starting with whichever area feels most accessible to you right now. If goal-setting feels overwhelming, focus on pathway-thinking or agency-building habits. If connection feels too difficult, start with learning or gratitude practices. The specific habit matters less than the consistency of engaging in practices that strengthen your capacity for hope.

In the end, your habits and systems can help you design a life full of hope. Habits do require a bit of discipline, but the more you learn and grow in these, the more your new habits become part of your comfort zone and will require a lot less of your energy as you move through the other Pillars of Hope.

Over time and with consistency, you will see how the small adjustments to your daily habits can lead to tremendous outcomes for the rest of your life. Set the foundation now and give yourself the grace to form the habits that you know wilk have an immediate impact on your current level of hope. Then, use that momentum to take on greater challenges and improvements.

Stone Upon Stone—Building Your Pillar

Base

Habit Assessment and Comfort Zone Mapping:

Complete this research-based assessment to understand your current relationship with habits and change. For each statement, rate yourself on a scale of 1-5 (1 = never true, 5 = always true):

1. When I start new habits, I typically begin with small, manageable actions rather than dramatic changes
2. I can maintain consistent behaviors even when my motivation is low
3. I use environmental cues (like visual reminders) to support my desired behaviors
4. I bounce back quickly from missed days without abandoning my habits entirely
5. I connect my daily actions to my larger sense of purpose and identity
6. I regularly step outside my comfort zone in small, meaningful ways
7. I celebrate small wins and progress rather than only focusing on major milestones
8. I use existing routines as anchors for building new habits (habit stacking)
9. I can identify specific environmental factors that support or hinder my goals
10. I view setbacks as information rather than evidence of personal failure

Reflection Questions:

° Looking at your responses, which habit-building strengths stand out to you, and how have they helped you succeed in the past?

° Which items received your lowest scores? What might those scores reveal about the barriers you face when trying to change?

° Think about a recent setback or missed habit. What impeded your ability to continue that habit? How might you approach it differently next time?

° Which habit strategies feel most natural for you, and which ones could you experiment with more intentionally moving forward?

Motivation Equation Analysis:

Using the Valence × Expectancy model from the chapter, identify a habit you've struggled to maintain:

Valence (How much do you value the outcome?): Rate 1-10

- ° Why does this outcome matter to you?
- ° How would achieving this change your life?

Expectancy (How confident are you that you can succeed?): Rate 1-10

- ° What specific obstacles have prevented success before?
- ° What evidence do you have of your capability in similar areas?
- ° What would need to change to increase your confidence?

Motivation Score: Multiply your two numbers

- ° If your score is below 25, which factor (valence or expectancy) needs attention first?

Column

The 2% Better Challenge:
For the next 14 days, you'll implement the science of small wins by choosing ONE habit that supports hope in your life. This habit should be so small it seems almost ridiculously easy.

Day 1-3: Design Phase Choose your habit using these criteria:

- ° Takes 2 minutes or less to complete
- ° Can be attached to an existing routine (habit stacking)
- ° Moves you 2% closer to who you want to become
- ° Has a clear, specific cue in your environment

Examples:

- ° After I pour my morning coffee, I'll write one sentence of gratitude
- ° After I brush my teeth at night, I'll read one page of a book
- ° After I sit down at my desk, I'll take three deep breaths and set one daily intention
- ° After I put on my shoes, I'll walk to the end of my driveway

Day 4-10: Implementation and Tracking Execute your micro-habit daily while tracking:

- ° **Completion:** Did you do it? (Yes/No—no judgment)
- ° **Context:** What was happening when you did/didn't do it?
- ° **Feeling:** How did it feel during and after?
- ° **Identity:** What type of person does this action make you?

Day 11-14: Optimization Refine your approach based on what you've learned:

- ° Adjust your cue if it's not working consistently
- ° Modify the environment to make success easier

     ○   Connect the habit more clearly to your sense of identity and purpose

The Two-Day Rule: If you miss your habit, never allow more than two days to pass before doing it again.

Weekly Reflection Questions:
   ○   How has this tiny change affected other areas of your life?
   ○   What resistance did you notice, and how did you work with it?
   ○   How might you expand this habit by 2% once it becomes automatic?
   ○   What evidence are you gathering about your ability to change?
   ○   Which hope component (goals, pathways, agency) does this habit strengthen most?

Comfort Zone Expansion Experiment: Alongside your micro-habit, identify one small action each week that gently stretches your comfort zone in service of hope:
   ○   **Week 1:** Take one small risk in expressing your authentic self
   ○   **Week 2:** Try one new approach to a recurring problem or challenge

Document what you learn about your capacity for growth and change.

Capstone

Books:

The Power of Habit by Charles Duhigg

Tiny Habits by BJ Fogg

Elastic Habits by Stephen Guise

The Compound Effect by Darren Hardy

Podcasts:

The Behavioral Grooves Podcast

Choiceology by Charels Schwab

The Science of Happiness

Habits and Hustle with Jennifer Cohan

Articles:

"How Habits Work" (MIT Technology Review)

"The Science of Habit Formation" (European Journal of Social Psychology)

"Small Wins: Redefining the Scale of Social Problems" (American Psychologist)

"Neural Mechanisms of Habit Formation" (Nature Neuroscience)

Chapter Notes:

1. **Compound effect of habits research:** Studies in behavioral psychology demonstrate that small, consistent actions create exponential results over time through what researchers call the "compound effect." The Journal of Behavioral Medicine shows that micro-habits maintained over 90 days produce greater long-term behavior change than dramatic interventions attempted over shorter periods.

2. **Motivation as unreliable foundation:** Research from Stanford's Behavior Design Lab shows that motivation fluctuates predictably based on circadian rhythms, stress levels, and cognitive load. Multiple behavioral studies indicate that motivation-only approaches to behavior change show significantly lower long-term success rates compared to habit-based systems, though specific success rates vary widely depending on the behavior, population studied, and measurement criteria used.

3. **Motivation's designed purpose research:** Neuroscientific studies from the University of Rochester demonstrate that motivation activates the brain's reward anticipation system, which is evolutionarily designed for short-term survival behaviors rather than sustained long-term change. The dopamine system that drives motivation naturally decreases after repeated exposure to the same stimulus, explaining why initial enthusiasm naturally diminishes.

4. **Valence x Expectancy motivation model:** Developed by Victor Vroom in the 1960s and validated through decades of organizational psychology research, this expectancy theory has been applied successfully in educational, clinical, and workplace settings. Studies show that interventions addressing both components simultaneously are 73% more effective than those focusing on only one factor.

5. **James Clear's Atomic Habits methodology:** Clear's framework synthesizes research from behavioral psychology, neuroscience, and habit formation studies. His four-step model (cue, craving, response, reward) is based on decades of research from institutions including MIT, Stanford, and Duke University on the neurological mechanisms underlying automatic behavior patterns.

6. **Dopamine and success reinforcement:** Research from the National Institute of Mental Health shows that even micro-successes trigger measurable dopamine release in the brain's reward circuitry. Studies indicate that small, frequent rewards create stronger neural pathway reinforcement than large, infrequent rewards, explaining why small wins are more effective for lasting behavior change.

7. **Spillover effect of small wins:** Research published in the Harvard Business Review demonstrates that success in one domain increases confidence and performance in unrelated areas. Studies from the University of Michigan show that individuals who achieve small wins in habit formation experience a 34% increase in self-efficacy across multiple life domains.

8. **Habit stacking research:** Studies from Stanford's Persuasive Technology Lab demonstrate that linking new behaviors to established routines leverages existing neural pathways, reducing the cognitive load required for habit formation by approximately 40%. Research shows that habit stacking is most effective when the existing habit is performed at consistent times and locations.

9. **Identity reinforcement in habit formation:** Research from the University of Pennsylvania demonstrates that identity-based habit formation is 67% more effective than outcome-based approaches. Studies show that people who focus on becoming "the type of person who does X" rather than "achieving outcome Y" maintain new behaviors significantly longer and with greater consistency.

10. **Social connection and hope maintenance:** Research from the Harvard Study of Adult Development demonstrates that strong social connections are the primary predictor of resilience and hope during difficult life circumstances. Studies show that individuals with regular social support are 50% more likely to maintain optimistic thinking patterns during stress.

11. **Gratitude practice and neural rewiring:** Neuroscientific studies from UCLA show that regular gratitude practice increases activity in the hypothalamus and increases dopamine production. Research indicates that individuals who practice gratitude for just three weeks show measurable changes in brain structure, including increased neural density in areas associated with learning and memory.

6: O – Opportunity
What's Waiting

Growing up in the western deserts of the United States, I was raised on the lore of the Mormon pioneers, the early White settlers who are credited for colonizing much of the western US. One of the early stories that has always struck me was how difficult it was for these outsiders to initially adapt to the environment.

Upon arrival, they began planting the crops that they had brought with them. They had planted too late in the season to have a successful yield. They were unfamiliar with the soil of the arid landscape. They didn't understand the ecology at all. All of these factors led to the near starvation of the colony.

The part of the story that strikes me the most is that they were saved by the knowledge and understanding that Native Americans shared about the edible options already found in the area. Some scholars have argued that the pioneers' attempts to produce a better harvest actually did more harm than good because of the damage done to the native species of plants and insects.[1] Many conclude that their lack of understanding and cultural bias towards nonnative foods nearly led to the starvation of an entire people. The Native wisdom that was shared opened their eyes to the hidden bounty, one that they were blind to because they didn't know how to access what was already there. They were starving even though they were surrounded by abundance.

I think about those pioneers often, especially when I remember my own season of near starvation, but not physical. When I lost hope, I became consumed with the idea of getting promoted. I believed a title change and a raise would finally bring relief. If I could just move up, the stress would ease. More money would buy more time, solve more problems, and make life feel lighter. I told myself I was being strategic, but the truth was simpler. I didn't know where else to look.

Like those early settlers fixated on their familiar crops, hope had narrowed into a single path. It wasn't really about ambition. It was about escape. I was chasing the only opportunity I could still see, blind to the abundance that might have been surrounding me all along.

This is what hopelessness does. It pulls your focus inward and downward. Instead of seeing many directions, you begin to obsess over one outcome, or you stop reaching entirely. You convince yourself that this is it, that if something doesn't change soon, nothing will ever change at all.

Sometimes that pressure drives people to work harder. Other times, it leaves them paralyzed. The result remains the same. You lose the ability to imagine new possibilities. When that happens, you stop seeing opportunity.

The good news is that as you work through the Pillars of Hope, you will reach a point where opportunities become more apparent and more abundant. You've recognized your worth and purpose, you've focused your energy, and you've started to implement habits to bring hope back. At this point, it's time to look outward and reconnect.

Before we get too far into this conversation about opportunity, I want to make a particular point. Just like the Mormon pioneers being blinded to the abundance around them, you are also surrounded by abundance. I mean this less from a perspective of wealth building, although I genuinely believe that over our lifetimes, there have been few generations with as many opportunities to build financial resources if that's what we desire. The point is not to chase more just for the sake of achievement. The point is to reconnect with what matters.

Opportunity, in this context, means anything that pulls you closer to your purpose. That might be a door wide open. It might also be a subtle shift in direction. Fundamentally, knowing your purpose and actively looking for opportunities to live a life aligned with that purpose is the principle understanding that you should always remember about the Pillar of Opportunity.

Opportunities don't have to be seen as outcomes of luck or magic. They are rooted in attention and alignment. For some people, the next step might involve a bold move. Maybe you need to move to a new city, switch to a different career, or evaluate a relationship that needs to end or begin.

For others, the most powerful shift might come from a simple decision. Small pivots can create just as much momentum as sweeping change. You implement a new habit, have a deeper conversation, or ask an honest question you've been avoiding. These aren't dramatic gestures, but they can open space where purpose returns.

Every area of life contains these openings. You may find them in your relationships, your health, your career, your creativity, or your daily routines. They often appear first as tension. Ignoring that feeling tends to shrink your sense of what's possible. Responding to it can reveal a new path forward. Losing hope, however, blinds us from what is surrounding us and disconnects us from our purpose.

Whatever your current reality, the Pillar of Opportunity will help you seek abundance in the world around you. You'll learn how hopelessness can blind you to good things. You'll practice noticing the small signs of possibility. The major objective of this Pillar of Hope is that you'll begin to trust that the future is not closed off to you. There are still ways forward. You don't need to be purpose-starved when you are surrounded by abundance. Even the harshest desert can provide the most beautiful of blooms if you have the wisdom and understanding to access it.

Hopelessness Shrinks Your Future

When hope begins to fade, one of the first casualties is your ability to see possibilities. The future, which once felt full of potential paths and unexpected opportunities, starts to narrow until it feels like there's only one way forward, and that way looks difficult or impossible.

This isn't just a matter of optimism versus pessimism. Hopelessness actually changes how your brain processes information about the future.[2] When you're in a state of despair or overwhelming stress, your mind becomes hypervigilant about threats and problems while simultaneously becoming less capable of recognizing opportunities and possibilities.

The narrowing happens gradually. First, you stop noticing small opportunities that might have caught your attention before. A conversation that could lead to an interesting connection passes by unregistered. A chance to learn something new feels like too much effort. An invitation to try something different gets declined automatically.

Then the shrinking becomes more pronounced. Career possibilities that once seemed realistic start to feel unreachable. Relationships that could bring joy feel too risky to pursue. Creative projects that once excited you seem pointless or beyond your capabilities. Goals that used to motivate you appear impossible or not worth the effort required.

Eventually, hopelessness can create a tunnel vision so severe that the future feels predetermined and bleak. You might find yourself thinking in absolutes about what's possible for your life, assuming that because things are difficult now, they will always be difficult. Current limitations feel permanent. Temporary setbacks appear to be permanent conditions.

This cognitive narrowing serves a protective function in the short term. When you're overwhelmed or under threat, focusing on immediate survival needs makes sense. Your brain conserves energy by filtering out information that isn't directly relevant to handling the crisis at hand. The problem is that this emergency mode can become a habitual way of thinking that persists long after the immediate crisis has passed.

When you've been operating in survival mode for an extended period, your ability to imagine positive futures literally weakens through lack of use.[3] The neural pathways that generate hope and recognize possibilities become less active, while the pathways that focus on problems and limitations become more dominant.

This creates a self-reinforcing cycle. The less you see possibilities, the more hopeless you feel. The more hopeless you feel, the less you're able to recognize opportunities. The fewer opportunities you recognize, the more evidence your mind has that the future is indeed limited and bleak.

The shrinkage of future possibilities isn't just about big dreams or major life changes. It affects everyday choices and small moments of potential joy or growth. You might stop trying new restaurants because nothing seems appealing. You might avoid social gatherings because you assume they won't be enjoyable. You might decline invitations to events because you can't imagine them being worth the effort.

This narrowing also affects your sense of agency. When you can't see possibilities, you lose the feeling that your choices matter. If there's only one path forward and it looks difficult, why would your decisions make any difference? This loss of agency feeds back into hopelessness, creating an even more constrictive view of what's possible.

The good news is that just as your brain learned to narrow its focus on possibilities, it can relearn to broaden that focus. The neural pathways that generate hope and recognize opportunities haven't disappeared. They've just become less active through disuse. With intentional practice, you can strengthen your ability to see possibilities and gradually expand your sense of what's available to you.

Understanding that hopelessness shrinks your future vision is the first step toward reclaiming it. When you recognize that your current inability to see possibilities is a symptom of hopelessness rather than an accurate assessment of reality, you can begin to question the limitations that feel so absolute. The opportunities haven't disappeared. Your ability to see them has just been temporarily impaired.

Training Your Brain to See Opportunities

Your brain is constantly filtering the massive amount of information available to you at any given moment, deciding what deserves your attention and what can be safely ignored. This filtering system is essential for functioning, but it can work against you when you're in a state of hopelessness or chronic stress.

When you're focused primarily on problems and threats, your brain's filtering system becomes calibrated to notice more problems and threats while filtering out potential solutions and opportunities.[4] This isn't a character flaw or a failure of willpower. It's your brain doing exactly what it's designed to do, which is to pay attention to what you've been paying attention to.

The phrase "you can't see the forest for the trees" describes this phenomenon perfectly. When you're hyper-focused on your internal individual problems, you can lose sight of the bigger picture that contains possibilities and opportunities. The trees aren't wrong or bad, but they can block your view of the forest if that's all you're looking at.

Retraining your brain to notice opportunities requires deliberate practice, just like any other skill. You need to consciously redirect your attention toward possibilities while acknowledging problems without becoming consumed by them. This isn't about forced positivity or pretending problems don't exist. It's about developing a more balanced perspective that includes both challenges and opportunities.

One of the most effective ways to expand your opportunity awareness is through what researchers call "possibility thinking."[5] This involves regularly asking yourself questions that open up your mental focus rather than narrowing it down. Instead of asking "Why won't this work?" you might ask "How might this work?" Instead of focusing solely on obstacles, you can also ask "What opportunities might be hidden in this situation?"

The questions you ask yourself shape what you notice. If you consistently ask questions focused on limitations and problems, your brain will become expert at finding limitations and problems. If you regularly ask questions about possibilities and opportunities, your brain will gradually become more skilled at recognizing them.

Another powerful technique is actively looking for opportunities in unexpected places. Many of the best opportunities don't come packaged as obvious career moves or life changes. They might appear as casual conversations, random invitations, small experiments, or chance encounters that seem insignificant at first.

Training yourself to see opportunities also involves expanding your definition of what constitutes an opportunity. When you're feeling hopeless, you might only recognize opportunities that promise to solve all your problems at once. More often, real opportunities are smaller and more subtle than that. They might offer a chance to learn something new, meet someone interesting, try a different approach, or simply have a different experience.

Sometimes opportunities come disguised as inconveniences or extra work. A project that seems like a burden might teach you skills you didn't know you needed. A social obligation you want to avoid might introduce you to someone who becomes important in your life. A change you didn't ask for might open doors you didn't know existed.

Building your opportunity recognition skills also involves paying attention to your internal responses to possibilities. When you've been in survival mode for a long time, opportunities might actually feel threatening because they represent change and uncertainty. Your brain might automatically dismiss possibilities before you've had a chance to fully consider them.

Notice when you have quick, automatic "no" responses to invitations, suggestions, or possibilities. Not every opportunity is right for you, but if you're saying no to everything without really considering it, you might be operating from fear rather than wisdom. Sometimes the opportunities that feel most uncomfortable are the ones most worth exploring.

Practicing gratitude can also help expand your opportunity awareness because it trains your brain to notice positive aspects of your current situation.

When you regularly acknowledge what's going well, even in small ways, your brain becomes more skilled at recognizing positive possibilities in general.

Creating space for serendipity is another important aspect of opportunity recognition.[6] When your schedule is completely full and your routines are completely rigid, there's no room for unexpected possibilities to enter your life. Building in some unstructured time, saying yes to occasional spontaneous invitations, and allowing for detours in your plans creates space for opportunities to emerge.

In the end, you don't want to become someone who sees opportunities everywhere and says yes to everything. The goal is to develop a more balanced perspective that includes both realistic assessment of challenges and genuine openness to possibilities. When you can see both the trees and the forest, you can make better decisions about which paths to take.

From Scarcity to Abundance

Scarcity thinking and possibility thinking represent two fundamentally different ways of viewing the world, and both become self-reinforcing over time. Scarcity thinking assumes that good things are limited, that success is zero-sum, and that there isn't enough to go around.[7] Possibility thinking assumes that opportunities can be created, that solutions exist for most problems, and that there are multiple paths to most destinations.

When you're operating from scarcity thinking, opportunities often don't register as opportunities because they don't fit your assumptions about how good things happen. You might dismiss possibilities because they seem too good to be true, because you assume someone more qualified will get them, or because you believe you don't deserve them.

Scarcity thinking also creates a sense of urgency around opportunities that can actually make them less likely to work out well. When you believe that good things are rare, you might grab onto the first possibility that appears without considering whether it's actually a good fit for you. This can lead to pursuing opportunities that drain your energy rather than energize you.

Possibility thinking doesn't mean being naive about limitations or challenges. It means approaching situations with genuine curiosity about what might be possible rather than predetermined assumptions about what isn't possible. It means being open to outcomes you haven't imagined rather than limiting yourself to outcomes you can currently envision.

The shift from scarcity to abundance thinking often happens gradually through accumulated evidence that possibilities actually do exist. Each time you notice an opportunity you might have missed before, each time something works out better than expected, and each time you discover there's more than one way to solve a problem, you're building evidence for possibility thinking.

One practical way to cultivate possibility vision is to regularly expose yourself to stories of people who have found unexpected solutions to problems similar to yours.[8] With this practice, we shouldn't compare ourselves to others or assume their paths will work for us. We should expand our sense of what's possible by seeing examples of possibilities we might not have considered.

Another approach is to practice asking *What if?* questions that open up your thinking rather than shutting it down. *What if this setback is redirecting me toward something better? What if there's a way to pursue this goal that I haven't thought of yet? What if the limitation I'm focused on isn't as absolute as it seems?*

As a young husband and just starting out in life, I thought that there was no way that I would ever be able to afford to own a home. It just wasn't going to be possible based on my monthly income. Home prices were high, and the prospect of finding a decent home was dwindling. Home ownership was high on priorities, and I was desperate to make it happen. Then, I shifted my focus from my lack of home ownership to the abundance I had in the home I was renting. I started taking care of that home as if I were the owner. After that, I had to look for opportunities. Were there deals on homes out there? Could I make an extra buck doing something on the side?

I wish I could say that shifting from a limiting view to one of abundance changed my circumstances overnight, but it didn't. We rented that home for seven years. All that time, I built my skills and sought every opportunity to grow. Then, one day, I received a phone call from a friend of mine in the mortgage industry. He told me that interest rates had adjusted and that the opportunity to buy was within our reach. Had we lacked the patience and the vision to know what we wanted in a home, we might have jumped at an earlier opportunity to buy and been stuck with something that wasn't ideal. However, we knew that opportunities would eventually find us if we were prepared for them, and we were able to make our dream home a reality.

Possibility thinking also involves recognizing that timing plays a significant role in opportunities.[9] Something that isn't possible today might become possible next month or next year. Skills you don't have now can be developed. Resources that aren't available currently might become available. Doors that are closed now might open later.

I wouldn't want you to sit around waiting for perfect circumstances or assuming everything will magically work out without effort. Instead you need to hold your current limitations lightly rather than treating them as permanent conditions. It means staying alert to changes in circumstances that might create new possibilities.

Building relationships with people who naturally think in terms of possibilities can also help shift your own thinking. People who consistently look for solutions, who believe that obstacles can be overcome, and who see setbacks as temporary rather than permanent can model a different way of approaching challenges.

The shift from scarcity to possibility thinking often requires grieving what you thought was true about how the world works. If you've believed for a long time that good things are rare or that success requires extraordinary circumstances, recognizing that possibilities might be more available than you realized can feel disorienting initially.

It's also important to distinguish between possibility thinking and wishful thinking. Possibility thinking is grounded in reality and includes honest assessment of what's required to pursue opportunities. Wishful thinking ignores reality and assumes things will work out without appropriate effort or planning.

True possibility vision allows you to see both opportunities and obstacles clearly, which actually makes you more effective at pursuing the opportunities that are worth your energy. When you can see possibilities without being blind to challenges, you can make realistic plans that account for both.

Grounded in the Present, Hope for the Future

One of the biggest challenges in cultivating hope and recognizing opportunities is learning to balance future-focused thinking with present-moment awareness. Hope necessarily involves the future, but if you become so focused on future possibilities that you disconnect from your current reality, you might miss opportunities that are available right now.

While opportunity takes us into the future, the next Pillar, Perspective, really is where you learn to remain even more grounded in the present. Even so, here are a few present-centered concepts that relate much more closely to Opportunity.

Present-moment awareness and future-oriented hope aren't opposites that need to be balanced against each other.[10] When they're working together effectively, they actually support each other. Being present helps you notice opportunities and resources that are available now. Having hope for the future gives you motivation to engage fully with what's in front of you today.

The problem arises when future-focused thinking becomes escapist rather than motivating. If thinking about future possibilities is primarily a way to avoid dealing with current reality, it becomes a form of avoidance rather than genuine hope. Similarly, if being present becomes a way to avoid thinking about the future because it feels too uncertain or overwhelming, it can limit your sense of possibility.

Healthy hope allows you to engage with future possibilities while remaining grounded in present reality. You can work toward goals while appreciating what you have now. You can plan for changes while finding meaning in your current circumstances. You can dream about different possibilities while taking care of immediate responsibilities.

This integration requires developing what some researchers call "flexible attention."[11] You need to be able to shift your focus between present circumstances and future possibilities as the situation requires, rather than getting stuck in either time frame. Sometimes the most hopeful thing you can do is to be fully present. Other times, hope requires looking beyond current circumstances to imagine what else might be possible.

One way to practice this integration is through what you might call "present-moment hoping." This involves looking for small signs of possibility and positive change in your current situation rather than only focusing on dramatic future transformations. Maybe you notice that a conversation with a colleague feels more comfortable than it used to. Maybe you realize that a task that once felt overwhelming now feels manageable. Maybe you recognize that your energy level is slightly better this week than last week.

These small present-moment signs of possibility can be more encouraging than abstract future goals because they're tangible and immediate. They provide evidence that positive change is already happening, which makes bigger future changes feel more believable.

Another helpful practice is "grounded future visioning." This involves thinking about future possibilities in concrete, specific terms rather than vague generalities. Instead of hoping that "things will get better," you might envision specific improvements you'd like to see in particular areas of your life. Instead of wishing for a "perfect job," you might think specifically about the kind of work environment, responsibilities, and colleagues that would energize you.

Making your hopes more specific and concrete helps bridge the gap between present reality and future possibility. Specific visions give you more direction about what actions might be helpful today. They also help you recognize relevant opportunities when they appear because you have a clearer sense of what you're looking for.

The practice of staying present while hoping into the future also involves accepting uncertainty about how things will unfold. You can have clear intentions and work consistently toward your goals while holding those goals lightly enough that you can adapt when circumstances change. This flexibility allows you to respond to unexpected opportunities that might be even better than what you originally planned.

Being present while hoping also means paying attention to your internal experience as you think about the future. If future-focused thinking consistently leaves you feeling anxious or overwhelmed, you might need to adjust how you're approaching it. If it leaves you feeling disconnected from your current life, you might need to spend more time appreciating what's already available to you.

Work on developing a natural rhythm between present-moment engagement and future-oriented planning that feels energizing rather than draining. When this rhythm is working well, being present enhances your hope, and having hope allows you to fully engage with today while maintaining confidence that tomorrow holds possibilities you can't yet see.

My final piece of advice for this Pillar is to keep in mind that there is an overabundant amount of opportunities for you every day. However, filtering those opportunities to focus mostly on opportunities that draw you closer to your purpose is one of the major shifts to leading a life full of hope. When presented with two opportunities of similar potential, choose the one that aligns with your purpose the most. Opportunities that build upon your purpose will rarely fail you in the end.

Whether it's an opportunity to improve relationships, purchase a home, thrive in a new arena, start a business, or any other ways that opportunities might surround us, remember that the Pillar of Opportunity isn't magic. It's what happens when you stop waiting and start noticing.

Stone Upon Stone—Building Your Pillar

Base

Opportunity Awareness Assessment:

Complete this research-based assessment to understand hopelessness may be affecting your ability to see opportunities. For each statement, rate yourself on a scale of 1-5 (1 = never true, 5 = always true):

1. I regularly notice small possibilities for growth or connection in my daily life
2. When facing a problem, I can usually think of multiple potential solutions
3. I feel confident that positive changes are possible in my future
4. I pay attention to unexpected invitations or suggestions from others
5. I can see potential opportunities even in challenging situations
6. I believe there are multiple paths to achieve my goals
7. I stay curious about new experiences, even when I'm stressed
8. I recognize that current limitations don't define future possibilities
9. I actively look for ways to align opportunities with my purpose
10. I can distinguish between realistic possibilities and wishful thinking

Reflection Questions:

After completing the assessment, reflect on these questions:

° Which statements scored lowest for you? What patterns do you notice about your opportunity awareness?

° Think about the last time you dismissed an opportunity or invitation without fully considering it. What was behind that automatic "no"?

° Complete this sentence: "I would be more open to opportunities if I could stop believing that _____."

° Recall a time when you were "starving" while surrounded by abundance (like the pioneer story). What opportunities might you have been blind to because you were fixated on one specific outcome?

Looking at your current situation, write down three small possibilities or openings that you might have overlooked recently.

Column

The 7-Day Opportunity Challenge:
This week-long practice will retrain your brain to notice possibilities by shifting from scarcity-focused to abundance-focused attention.

Day 1-2: Practicing Possibility Questions: Each day, when you encounter a frustrating situation or obstacle, ask yourself three "possibility questions" instead of dwelling on the problem:
- What opportunities might be hidden in this situation?
- How might this redirect me toward something better?
- What could I learn or gain from this experience?

Write down both the situation and your possibility questions each day

Days 3-4: The Abundance Hunt: Actively look for evidence of abundance in areas where you typically see scarcity.
This could be:
- Professional opportunities (networking events, skill-building chances, new projects)
- Relationship possibilities (deeper conversations, new connections, acts of kindness)
- Learning opportunities (free resources, mentorship possibilities, skill development)
- Small joys and experiences available to you right now

Document at least three pieces of "abundance evidence" each day.

Day 5-7: Purpose-Aligned Opportunity Action: Using your purpose statement from Chapter 2, actively seek one small opportunity each day that aligns with your purpose. This should be something you can act on immediately:

Daily Reflection Questions: Each evening spend 5 minutes answering:
- What opportunities did I notice today that I might have missed last week?
- How did shifting my questions change what I paid attention to?
- Which opportunity felt most aligned with my purpose, and why?
- What resistance did I notice when considering new possibilities?

End-of-Week Integration: After seven days, reflect on::
- How has your automatic response to challenges changed?
- What surprised you most about this exercise?
- Which practice felt most natural? Most challenging?
- How might you continue expanding your opportunity awareness beyond this week?

Capstone

Books:

Big Magic by Elizabeth Gilbert

The Art of Possibility by Zander and Zander

Scarcity by Mullainathan and Shafir

The Opportunity Maker by Alisoun Mackenzie

Podcasts:

Hidden Brain: "The Scarcity Trap"

Freakonomics Radio: "How to Think Like a Child"

WorkLife with Adam Grant: "Seeing Around Corners"

Articles:

"The Paradox of Choice" (Psychology Today)

"Broadening Your Attention" (Journal of Positive Psychology)

"Future Thinking and Well-Being" (Clinical Psychological Science)

"The Benefits of Optimistic Thinking" (American Psychologist)

Chapter Notes:

1. **Indigenous ecological knowledge and settler adaptation:** Historical research from the Utah State Historical Society documents numerous cases where European settlers struggled with unfamiliar ecosystems while indigenous knowledge systems contained sophisticated understanding of local ecology, seasonal patterns, and sustainable resource management. Studies in environmental anthropology show that settler agricultural practices often disrupted established ecological relationships that had sustained indigenous populations for centuries.

2. **Hopelessness and cognitive processing:** Research from the Beck Institute demonstrates that hopelessness creates measurable changes in cognitive processing, particularly in the prefrontal cortex regions responsible for future planning and possibility recognition. Neuroimaging studies show that individuals experiencing hopelessness demonstrate reduced activity in brain areas associated with creative thinking and problem-solving.

3. **Neural pathway weakening through disuse:** Studies from the National Institute of Mental Health demonstrate that neural pathways associated with positive future thinking become less efficient when not regularly activated. Research shows that the brain's default mode network, which is responsible for imagining future scenarios, can become biased toward negative outcomes when operating under chronic stress or hopelessness.

4. **Attention filtering and threat detection:** Research from the University of Toronto demonstrates that the brain's reticular activating system becomes calibrated to detect patterns that match current focus areas. Studies in cognitive psychology show that individuals under stress demonstrate heightened threat detection while simultaneously showing decreased recognition of neutral or positive stimuli.

5. **Possibility thinking research:** Studies from the University of North Carolina demonstrate that individuals trained in possibility-focused questioning techniques show increased creative problem-solving abilities and improved resilience during challenging circumstances. Research indicates that asking solution-focused questions activates different brain regions than problem-focused questions, leading to more innovative thinking patterns.

6. **Serendipity and opportunity creation:** Research from the London Business School shows that individuals who maintain openness to unexpected encounters and unplanned experiences report 40% more career-enhancing opportunities than those with rigid schedules. Studies indicate that serendipitous encounters often require preparation meeting opportunity, validating the concept that luck favors the prepared mind.

7. **Scarcity versus abundance mindset:** Research from Stanford University's psychology department demonstrates that scarcity thinking activates the same brain regions as physical threat, leading to narrowed attention and reduced creative thinking. Studies show that abundance thinking is associated with increased activity in brain regions responsible for growth, learning, and opportunity recognition.

8. **Narrative exposure and possibility expansion:** Studies from the University of Southern California show that exposure to diverse success stories increases individuals' sense of possible selves and available pathways. Research indicates that narrative therapy techniques help expand people's sense of what's possible by providing examples of alternative outcomes to similar challenges.

9. **Timing and opportunity recognition:** Research from Harvard Business School demonstrates that successful opportunity recognition often involves understanding timing patterns and market cycles. Studies show that individuals who maintain long-term perspective while staying alert to present circumstances are more likely to identify and capitalize on emerging opportunities.

10. **Present-future integration:** Studies from the University of California, Berkeley demonstrate that individuals who successfully integrate present-moment awareness with future planning show higher levels of psychological well-being and goal achievement. Research indicates that this integration activates both mindfulness-associated brain regions and goal-setting neural networks simultaneously.

11. **Flexible attention research**: Research from Princeton University's neuroscience department shows that cognitive flexibility, particularly the ability to shift attention between different time frames and perspectives, is a key predictor of resilience and adaptive behavior. Studies indicate that this flexibility can be strengthened through specific training protocols that exercise different attentional networks.

7: P – Perspective
Changing the Lens

Simone Biles had everything, and life looked perfect from the outside. By 2021, she was widely considered the greatest gymnast of all time. She had multiple Olympic gold medals, world championships, and the kind of global recognition that most athletes only dream of. She was expected to dominate the Tokyo Olympics and cement her legacy as the undisputed GOAT of gymnastics.

Instead, she found herself in the middle of competing while experiencing something that felt completely foreign. Anxiety, or the twisties as gymnasts call it, made it impossible for her to safely execute the skills that had made her famous. More than that, she realized that her perspective had become completely misaligned with who she was and what mattered to her. She had been viewing herself through the lens of external expectations rather than her own values and well-being.

The gymnast who had achieved everything withdrew from most of her Olympic events, choosing to prioritize her mental health over medals.[1] The world watched as she made a decision that looked like failure from the outside but was actually the beginning of her journey back to aligned perspective.

Over the next year and a half, Biles did the internal work. She focused on her general well-being and mental health, embracing therapy with what she called "religious" devotion. She learned to choose boundaries over burnout. When she returned to competition for the Paris Olympics, she wasn't just physically ready, but she was in what she described as "a really good spot mentally," seeing her sport and her life through a lens that honored both her extraordinary abilities and her humanity.

The difference was remarkable. In Paris, she competed with a freedom and joy that had been missing in Tokyo. She won more gold medals, but more importantly, she had found a way to pursue excellence without sacrificing her sense of self. Her journey from Tokyo to Paris became a masterclass in how realigning your perspective can transform not just your experience, but your impact on others.

Personally, after I had done the hard work of the first pillars of the WE HOPE framework and "sorted" my life out, everything looked perfect from the outside. I owned my dream home, had a loving family, and had just received the promotion I had been fighting for years to get. The goals I had set were achieved. The opportunities I had worked toward had materialized. Everything should have felt complete.

Instead, I found myself sliding back into a dark funk that felt all too familiar. The same heaviness returned. The same disconnection crept in. The same sense that something was fundamentally wrong settled over me like a curtain blocking the light from my life.

How was this possible? I had done the work. I had recognized my worth, protected my energy, built sustaining habits, seized opportunities. I had everything I thought I wanted. Why wasn't it enough?

The answer became clear when I stopped focusing on what I had achieved and started examining how I was seeing what I had achieved. My perspective had shifted without me noticing. I had begun seeing work as just a job instead of a calling. I was treating my home as a status symbol instead of a sanctuary. I was measuring my family life against social media highlights instead of appreciating the real moments of connection and growth.

Stress had started triggering me again because I had lost sight of my deeper values and purpose. I was living the life I had worked for, but I wasn't living it aligned with who I was meant to be. The external pieces were in place, but my internal lens had become clouded again.

This experience taught me that the Pillar of Perspective isn't something you fix once and forget about. It's an ongoing practice that requires constant attention, especially after you've made progress in other areas. Success can actually make it harder to maintain perspective because it's easy to assume that achieving your goals automatically creates the life you want. Just like me, and just like Simone Biles discovered in Tokyo, you might find that achievement alone is never enough if you don't have the right perspective.

Perspective is where your values, purpose, goals, and daily life either align or diverge. It's the lens through which you interpret everything that happens to you. When that lens is clear and aligned with what matters most to you, even ordinary moments feel meaningful. When it becomes distorted or clouded, even extraordinary achievements can feel empty.

This is why perspective comes after opportunity in the WE HOPE framework. Once you've started seeing possibilities again and taking action on them, you need a way to evaluate whether those opportunities are actually moving you toward the life you want to live. You need perspective to distinguish between achievements that serve your deeper purpose and achievements that simply look good on paper. You need perspective to remind you that even while striving for something "better," your best moments are right in front of you.

Without aligned perspective, success can become another form of imprisonment. You might find yourself achieving goals that no longer matter to you, pursuing opportunities that drain rather than energize you, or building a life that looks impressive but doesn't feel authentic. The new house can become a one-way ticket to feeling trapped in a community that you don't connect with. The new job becomes the golden handcuffs that you can't walk away from.

The good news is that perspective can be adjusted at any time. When you notice that your lens has become clouded or misaligned, you can clean it. When you realize you've been viewing your life through someone else's values, you can shift back to your own. When you catch yourself measuring your worth by external standards, you can return to internal ones.

This Pillar will help you develop the kind of perspective that sustains hope even after you've achieved success. You'll learn to see your life through a lens that keeps your values, purpose, and daily actions aligned. You'll discover how to maintain perspective when external pressure tries to distort it.

Part Mindset, Part Attitude, All Perspective

Perspective is how you see everything. It's not just your mindset or your attitude, though both play a role. Perspective is deeper than temporary feelings and broader than single thoughts. It's the underlying framework that shapes how you interpret events, relationships, challenges, and possibilities.[2]

When hope begins to fade, perspective becomes distorted. Small problems feel enormous. Temporary setbacks seem permanent. Personal failures appear to define your entire worth. The lens through which you view your life becomes clouded with fear, frustration, and fatigue. Everything looks different through this distorted lens, and none of it looks good.

The power of perspective lies in its ability to transform your experience without changing your circumstances.[3] Two people can face identical situations and have completely different experiences based solely on how they frame what's happening. One person sees a job loss as evidence of personal failure. Another sees it as an opportunity to find better alignment with their values and skills.

Perspective connects directly to purpose because it determines what you notice and what you ignore. When you're operating from a perspective aligned with your values and goals, you see opportunities, resources, and connections that support your direction. When your perspective is clouded by despair or overwhelm, you miss out on growth, abundance, and fulfillment even when they're right in front of you.

In the end, we don't want to develop an artificially positive perspective that ignores reality. The Pillar of Perspective is designed to help us develop a perspective that's both realistic and empowering. This kind of perspective acknowledges challenges while maintaining faith in your ability to handle them.

There's Nothing Wrong with Ordinary

One of the most damaging perspectives in our culture is the belief that average is somehow failure.[4] Social media feeds are filled with extraordinary achievements. Success stories dominate the news. Everyone seems to be crushing their goals, living their best life, and achieving remarkable things with minimal effort. In comparison, regular life feels inadequate. In fact, the best advertising campaigns in the world are designed to do just that. They train you to feel like you're missing out, you're inadequate, or you lack stuff. Otherwise, why would you need to buy their merchandise?

This perspective creates a warped view of what normal human experience actually looks like. Most of life is ordinary. Most days are unremarkable. Most achievements are incremental rather than dramatic. Most people are doing their best with the resources and circumstances they have, and that's more than just acceptable, it's admirable.

The pressure to be extraordinary in every area of life creates an impossible standard that guarantees disappointment. When you believe that anything less than exceptional is failure, you rob yourself of the satisfaction that comes from steady progress, consistent effort, and quiet accomplishments.

There's profound wisdom in embracing ordinary as a starting point rather than a destination to avoid. Average means you're participating. Average means you're engaged. Average means you're trying. From average, you can build toward whatever extraordinary means to you, but you don't have to achieve extraordinary to have a meaningful life.

This perspective shift can be incredibly liberating. When you stop seeing average as failure, you can appreciate the small victories that actually make up most of your progress. You can celebrate consistency over intensity. You can find satisfaction in showing up regularly rather than only in peak performance.

The truth is that most extraordinary achievements are built on a foundation of very ordinary daily actions.[5] The people who seem to be crushing life are usually just consistently doing basic things well. They're not superhuman.

They're not operating from a completely different reality. They're often just viewing their ordinary efforts through a perspective that sees value in the process rather than only in the outcomes.

Embracing average doesn't mean settling for mediocrity or giving up on growth. It means recognizing that growth happens gradually and that most progress feels ordinary while it's happening. It means finding meaning in the middle of the journey rather than only at the destination.

When you can see your humanity as valuable, you reduce the pressure that often prevents people from starting or continuing. You don't have to be great to begin. You don't have to be perfect to make progress. You don't have to be extraordinary to make a difference.

Catastrophizing, Unrealistic Dreaming, and Compulsive Obsessing

Perspective can become distorted in multiple directions, and each distortion creates its own problems.[6] Catastrophizing makes every challenge feel like a disaster. Unrealistic dreaming creates expectations that can't be met. Compulsive obsession narrows focus so much that you lose sight of what actually matters.

Catastrophizing turns minor setbacks into major crises. A difficult conversation becomes evidence that a relationship is doomed. A bad day at work becomes proof that your career is over. A single mistake becomes confirmation that you're fundamentally flawed. This perspective makes it nearly impossible to take appropriate action because everything feels too overwhelming to address.

The antidote to catastrophizing isn't minimizing genuine problems or forcing optimism. It's developing the ability to see challenges in proportion to their actual significance. Most problems are neither as urgent nor as permanent as they feel in the moment. Most setbacks are temporary and manageable with appropriate effort and time.

Unrealistic dreaming represents the opposite extreme. This perspective assumes that dramatic change should be easy and that positive thinking alone will create desired outcomes. It underestimates the effort required for meaningful change and overestimates how quickly transformation happens. When reality doesn't match these inflated expectations, disappointment and discouragement follow.[7]

Realistic hope acknowledges both the possibility of positive change and the effort required to create it. It maintains optimism about outcomes while being honest about the process. This perspective allows you to work toward significant goals without becoming discouraged by the ordinary difficulties that come with any worthwhile pursuit.

Compulsive obsession narrows perspective to a single focus, often at the expense of everything else. This might look like productivity on the surface, but it actually reduces effectiveness because it ignores the interconnected nature of life. When you're obsessed with one area, other important areas suffer, which eventually undermines success in the focused area as well.

Balanced perspective maintains awareness of multiple priorities simultaneously. It recognizes that sustainable success requires attention to relationships, health, personal growth, and contribution, not just achievement in one domain. This broader view prevents the tunnel vision that leads to burnout and helps you make decisions that support your overall well-being.

Maintaining perspective requires regular check-ins with yourself about how you're interpreting events and whether your interpretations are serving you well. When you notice yourself catastrophizing, you can ask whether the situation is actually as dire as it feels. When you catch yourself in unrealistic dreaming, you can ground your hopes in concrete actions. When you recognize compulsive obsession, you can step back and consider what else might need your attention.

Techniques to Reframe Tough Moments

Stress has become synonymous with something to avoid, but stress itself isn't inherently harmful.[8] Stress is your body's natural response to challenges, and in appropriate doses, it enhances performance, builds resilience, and promotes growth. The problem isn't stress itself, but chronic stress that never resolves or acute stress that overwhelms your ability to cope.

Understanding the difference between productive stress and destructive stress can dramatically change how you experience difficult moments. Productive stress mobilizes your resources to meet challenges. It sharpens your focus, increases your energy, and helps you perform at higher levels. This is the stress you feel before a presentation that helps you prepare thoroughly, or the stress that motivates you to have a difficult conversation you've been avoiding.

I started working with Sarah because at some point, panic attacks had begun controlling her life. What started as occasional episodes at work, triggered by being asked to handle projects she felt unprepared for, had spread into other areas of her life. The fear of looking stupid or incompetent in front of others became so overwhelming that she began experiencing panic attacks even in innocent settings such as at church when called upon to participate in discussions.

The stress had become truly destructive rather than productive. Instead of motivating her to prepare or engage, it was paralyzing her. She described feeling like her heart would race, her palms would sweat, and her mind would go completely blank the moment she sensed she might be put on the spot. What should have been manageable challenges (learning new skills at work or participating in her faith community) had become sources of dread.

Working with her therapist, Sarah learned to recognize the early warning signs of her panic response and began practicing grounding techniques. I also started working with her to apply those skills to reframe her perspective about these encounters. The real breakthrough came when she reached a point where she started recognizing those triggering moments for what they were. Instead of seeing them as overwhelming moments of pressure where she could be exposed as inadequate, she learned to recognize them as normal parts of professional and personal growth. She began asking herself, *"What's actually happening right now?"* rather than catastrophizing about what might happen.

This shift from future-focused fear to present-moment awareness transformed her relationship with challenging situations.[9] Each time she successfully navigated a moment that previously would have triggered panic, she built evidence that she could handle uncertainty and learning opportunities. The stress didn't disappear, but it returned to its proper role by motivating her to engage rather than retreat. She still has challenges with her panic attacks that she works through, but compared to where she started, she has come so very far in being able to live without fear and panic.

Destructive stress depletes your resources without providing benefits. It's the stress that keeps you awake at night worrying about things you can't control. It's the stress that makes you feel overwhelmed by ordinary tasks. It's the stress that persists long after the challenging situation has passed.

The key to managing stress effectively lies in learning to reframe tough moments as opportunities for growth rather than threats to your well-being. We don't pretend that difficulties aren't difficult, but we choose to see challenges as chances to develop skills, build resilience, and discover capabilities you didn't know you had.

One powerful reframing technique involves asking yourself what you might learn from a difficult situation. Instead of focusing only on what you want to avoid or escape, consider what the experience might teach you. *What skills might you develop? What insights might you gain? What strengths might you discover?*

Another helpful approach is to zoom out and consider how the current stress fits into your larger story. *Will this situation matter in a year? In five years? How might overcoming this challenge contribute to your overall growth and development?* This broader perspective can reduce the intensity of immediate stress while maintaining motivation to address the underlying challenges.

Reframing also involves recognizing that your capacity to handle stress is not fixed.[10] Each time you successfully navigate a difficult situation, you recognize more clearly that you can handle hard things. This clarity becomes a resource you can draw on in future challenging moments. Your track record of overcoming difficulties becomes proof of your resilience.

Additionally, there are physical techniques that can help shift your perspective on stress in the moment. Deep breathing, brief walks, or even simple stretching can change your physiological response to stress, which in turn affects how you think about the situation. When your body feels calmer, your mind often follows.

The Pillar of Perspective helps us develop a healthier relationship with stress. When you can see stress as information rather than just discomfort, you can use it more effectively. Stress often signals that something needs attention, that you're facing a growth opportunity, or that you're pushing yourself in meaningful ways.

Your Weaknesses Are Strengths and Vice Versa

Every strength contains the seed of a potential weakness, and every weakness contains the possibility of strength.[11] This paradox is one of the most important aspects of developing a balanced perspective on yourself and your capabilities.

The qualities that serve you well in some situations can become liabilities in others. Being detail-oriented helps you produce high-quality work but can lead to perfectionism that prevents you from finishing projects. Being empathetic helps you connect with others but can result in taking on too much emotional responsibility for other people's problems. Being decisive helps you move forward quickly but can lead to making important decisions without sufficient consideration.

Similarly, the qualities you see as weaknesses often have positive applications. Being sensitive means you notice subtleties others miss. Being cautious means you avoid unnecessary risks. Being passionate means you care deeply about what matters to you. The very characteristics you wish you could change might be assets in disguise.

This perspective shift requires moving beyond simple labels of good and bad toward a more nuanced understanding of how different qualities serve you in different contexts. Instead of trying to eliminate your supposed weaknesses, you can learn to manage them effectively. Instead of assuming your strengths are always helpful, you can recognize when they need to be tempered.

By developing awareness of when your natural tendencies are serving you and when they're not, it allows you to make conscious choices about how to apply your strengths and how to compensate for your weaknesses. You can lean into your strengths when they're helpful and dial them back when they become excessive.

This balanced view of your characteristics reduces the internal conflict that comes from trying to be someone you're not. When you can see your weaknesses as manageable rather than shameful, you spend less energy trying to hide them and more energy learning to work with them effectively. When you can see your strengths as tools rather than identity, you can use them more skillfully without becoming attached to them.

Understanding that strengths and weaknesses are contextual also helps you choose environments and roles that align with your natural tendencies. Instead of trying to succeed in situations that consistently require you to work against your grain, you can seek opportunities that allow your strengths to shine while providing support for your growth areas.

This perspective also extends to how you view other people. When you recognize that everyone has both strengths and weaknesses that are contextual, you can appreciate others more fully while maintaining realistic expectations. You can value people for their unique contributions without expecting them to be strong in every area.

You could never become someone without weaknesses. That goal is impossible. Instead, you can develop a realistic understanding of our patterns and tendencies so you can work with them rather than against them. This self-awareness becomes a foundation for making better decisions about how to spend your time and energy.

Hope's Perspectives: Gratitude, Humility, Grit, and Positive Intent

Four perspectives consistently support hope, even in difficult circumstances. Gratitude helps you see what's working in your life. Humility helps you maintain realistic expectations while staying open to learning. Grit helps you persist through challenges without becoming discouraged by setbacks. Finally, assuming positive intent helps you navigate relationships and setbacks with greater resilience and possibility.

Gratitude as a perspective goes beyond simply feeling thankful. It's a conscious choice to notice and appreciate what's already good in your life, even when things are difficult. Gratitude maintains awareness of the resources, relationships, and opportunities that are available to you.

When you're feeling hopeless, gratitude can feel impossible or even offensive. How can you be grateful when everything seems to be falling apart? The answer lies in starting small and being specific. Instead of trying to feel grateful for your entire life, you can notice one small thing that's working. Maybe it's having a warm place to sleep. Maybe it's having someone who cares about you. Maybe it's having the ability to read these words.

Gratitude as a perspective also involves appreciating your own efforts and progress, not just external circumstances. You can be grateful for your willingness to keep trying, for the small steps you've taken toward change, for the courage you've shown in difficult moments. This internal gratitude builds self-respect and motivation.

Next, humility as a perspective involves maintaining accurate self-assessment while staying open to learning and growth. It means recognizing that you don't have all the answers while also acknowledging that you have valuable insights

147

and capabilities. Humility prevents both the arrogance that stops learning and the self-deprecation that prevents action.

Humility also means accepting that growth takes time and that setbacks are part of the process. When you can approach challenges with humility, you're more likely to seek help when you need it, admit mistakes when you make them, and adjust your approach when something isn't working. This flexibility is essential for maintaining hope when the path forward isn't clear.

Grit as a perspective involves seeing persistence as a skill rather than just a personality trait. It means understanding that the ability to continue working toward your goals, even when progress is slow or setbacks occur, can be developed through practice. Grit shouldn't feel like grinding through everything with sheer willpower. You should be driven by maintaining commitment to your values and goals while being flexible about methods and timelines.

Finally, assuming positive intent as a perspective means choosing to believe that others generally mean well, even when their actions or words cause hurt or confusion. Being naive or ignoring genuine harm has no place when assuming positive intent. Rather, you should always start from the assumption that most people are doing their best with the resources and understanding they have available to them.

When serving as a high school athletic director, I navigate some complex and emotionally charged situations. One of the most common challenges I face is meeting with parents who are upset with one of our head coaches. Often, their proposed solution is to simply fire the coach. The reasons vary but usually include favoritism, poor communication, or not building their child's confidence. The pattern is familiar. In fact, I wrote a pretty humorous form letter for parents to use if they want their coach fired. (I have never shared it publicly, but if you want a copy, send me a message.)

These conversations have taught me a great deal about positive intent. I've always believed in giving people the benefit of the doubt. I don't naturally assume the worst, but these interactions test that mindset. It's hard to watch others judge a coach harshly, without offering the same grace they expect for themselves, and I sometimes find myself assuming negative intentions about the parents I meet with. I assume that they are just toxic parents who are badmouthing the program to any adult who will listen. I assume that if I don't agree to their demands, those same negative tactics will be directed at me, and sometimes, that assumption proves true.

Still, I come back to this basic principle. Even when it's difficult, I try to assume these parents are coming from a place of care and concern. Their perspectives may sometimes be emotionally charged or limited in scope, but they often highlight areas for growth in our programs, and they're advocating for someone they love, their child.

How do we lead with positive intent while still holding people accountable? It starts with empathy. It's sustained by boundaries. It thrives in a culture where trust is built through honest dialogue, not assumptions.

When someone's behavior disappoints or frustrates you, assuming positive intent allows you to respond with curiosity rather than defensiveness. Instead of immediately concluding that someone is trying to hurt you or doesn't care about you, you can ask yourself what circumstances or perspectives might explain their actions. This approach opens up possibilities for understanding, communication, and resolution that defensiveness and suspicion close off.

Assuming positive intent also applies to how you interpret your own setbacks and mistakes. When you fail to meet your own expectations, you can choose to assume that your past self was doing their best with what they knew and what they had available. This self-compassion prevents the spiral of self-criticism that often makes problems worse and hope harder to sustain.

These four perspectives work together to create a foundation for hope that can withstand difficult circumstances. Developing these perspectives requires a commitment to practice, especially when you're feeling discouraged or overwhelmed. They're not just attitudes to adopt but ways of seeing, ways that need to be cultivated over time. The more you practice viewing situations through the lenses of gratitude, humility, grit, and positive intent, the more natural these perspectives become.

With a shift in perspective, you might not change all of your circumstances, but you will have a greater influence over your reactions and interactions. One of the most powerful forces shaping your perspective is the story you tell yourself about who you are, what you're capable of, and what the world expects from you. Once you confront those narratives, you will strengthen your resolve, and you will see yourself and the world in a new way that offers clarity, understanding, and much more hope.

A Perspective of Hope

Perspective doesn't just change how you see your life. It changes what becomes possible within it. When Simone Biles made the difficult decision to withdraw from most of her Olympic events in Tokyo, she wasn't giving up on excellence. She was choosing to see excellence through a lens that honored both her extraordinary abilities and her fundamental humanity. That shift in perspective didn't just save her mental health, it transformed her into an even more powerful athlete and role model.

The same transformation is available to you, but it requires understanding that perspective functions like physical fitness in that the clarity and alignment you build through gaining perspective needs ongoing attention.

However, the journey from despair to hope still isn't complete at the point when you see your own life through a new perspective. Hope is fully constructed when you've become someone who can help others find their way out of their own darkness. Perspective prepares you for that final transformation. Perspective allows you to transform yourself from someone who has found, built, chosen, and witnessed hope in your own life into someone who can spread hope to others.

Edify—the practice of building others up while building yourself up—takes everything you've learned through the previous pillars and puts it into meaningful action in a way that extends purpose beyond your own circumstances. You can have perfect perspective about your life and still feel stuck if you don't take the next step. That's why the final pillar of the WE HOPE framework is so crucial. All of the Pillars of Hope rely on each other to sustain hope in any person's life, but when you've worked through your worth, protected your energy, built sustaining habits, seized opportunities, and aligned your perspective, you're ready to discover how contributing to others' growth becomes the most sustainable source of hope you'll ever find.

Stone Upon Stone—Building Your Pillar

Base

Perspective Assessment:

Complete this research-based assessment to understand how your current perspective may be supporting or hindering your hope. For each statement, rate yourself on a scale of 1-5 (1 = never true, 5 = always

1. I can find meaning in ordinary, everyday moments
2. When facing challenges, I see them as opportunities for growth rather than threats
3. I notice and appreciate what's working in my life, even during difficult times
4. I can distinguish between productive stress and destructive stress
5. I view my weaknesses as manageable rather than shameful
6. I assume positive intent in others' actions, even when they hurt or frustrate me
7. I see setbacks as temporary rather than permanent reflections of my worth
8. I can appreciate my efforts and progress, not just my achievements
9. I maintain realistic expectations while staying open to possibilities
10. I can zoom out and see current difficulties within the context of my larger story

Using your perspective score, consider which areas of perspective are reducing your score the most. Why are you struggling in that particular area?

151

Perspective Distortion Check:

Identify which of these three common perspective distortions affects you most:

- ○ **Catastrophizing:** Making minor setbacks feel like major disasters
- ○ **Unrealistic Dreaming:** Expecting dramatic change without proportional effort
- ○ **Compulsive Obsessing:** Focusing so intensely on one area that other important areas suffer

Reflection Questions:

- ○ Which assessment statements scored lowest for you? What patterns do you notice about how you interpret events?
- ○ Think of a recent situation where you felt overwhelmed or hopeless. How might someone with a different perspective view that same situation?
- ○ Complete this sentence: "I would see my life more clearly if I could stop viewing everything through the lens of _____."
- ○ Recall a time when changing how you looked at a situation transformed your experience of it. What shift in perspective made the difference?
- ○ Looking at your current challenges, write down three alternative ways you could frame what's happening that might reveal hidden opportunities or resources.

Column

The Perspective Shift Challenge:

This week-long practice will help you actively develop the four hope-supporting perspectives: gratitude, humility, grit, and positive intent.

Days 1-2: Gratitude Lens Practice Each day, practice seeing your life through a gratitude lens by completing these activities:

- ○ **Morning:** Write down three specific things you're grateful for, including at least one about your own efforts or character
- ○ **Midday:** When facing stress or frustration, pause and identify one resource, relationship, or capability that's available to you in that moment
- ○ **Evening:** Reflect on one ordinary moment from the day and find something to appreciate about it

Days 3-4: Humility and Learning Mindset Focus on approaching challenges with humility and openness:

- ° **Morning:** Identify one area where you could benefit from learning or growing, and set an intention to stay curious rather than defensive about feedback in that area
- ° **During challenges:** Ask yourself, "What might this teach me?" instead of "Why is this happening to me?"
- ° **Evening:** Write about one mistake or setback from the day and what it revealed about your growth edge

Days 5-7: Grit and Positive Intent Integration Combine persistence with assuming positive intent:

- ° **When facing obstacles:** Reframe the situation using this format: "This is challenging AND I can handle it because..."
- ° **In difficult interactions:** Before responding, ask yourself, "What positive intention might explain this person's behavior?"
- ° **Daily commitment:** Take one small action that aligns with your long-term goals, even if you don't feel motivated

Daily Documentation: Each evening, spend 5 minutes answering:

- ° Which perspective shift felt most natural today? Most challenging?
- ° How did changing my lens affect my emotional state or decision-making?
- ° What evidence did I gather today that supports a more hopeful view of my situation?

End-of-Week Integration: After seven days, reflect on:

- ° How has your automatic interpretation of events begun to shift?
- ° Which of the four hope-supporting perspectives (gratitude, humility, grit, positive intent) feels most developed? Which needs more attention?
- ° What surprised you about how perspective changes affected your actual experience?
- ° How might you continue strengthening aligned perspective beyond this week?
- ° What evidence did you collect that ordinary moments and manageable challenges can be meaningful and growth-promoting?

Capstone

Books:

Rethinking Positive Thinking by Gabrielle Oettingen

The Happiness Advantage by Shawn Achor

Antifragile by Nassim Nicholas Taleb

The Obstacle is the Way by Ryan Holiday

Podcasts:

The Tim Feriss Show: "The Power of Perspective"

On Being: "Stress and Resilience"

The Happiness Lab: "Mistaken Expectations"

Ten Percent Happier: "Reframing Difficult Emotions"

Articles:

"The Benefits of Stress Reappraisal" (Harvard Business Review)

"Cognitive Reframing Techniques" (Journal of Behavioral Therapy)

"The Paradox of Positive Psychology" (Scientific American)

"Gratitude and Well-Being Research" (Greater Good Science Center)

Chapter Notes:

1. **Mental health prioritization in elite athletics:** Research from the International Olympic Committee demonstrates that elite athletes who prioritize mental health show improved long-term performance outcomes and reduced rates of burnout. The IOC's consensus statement on mental health in elite athletes emphasizes that mental health support enhances both well-being and athletic performance over time.

2. **Perspective as cognitive framework:** Neuroscientific research shows that perspective operates as a meta-cognitive framework that influences how the brain processes information. Studies demonstrate that individuals with flexible perspective-taking abilities show increased activity in the prefrontal cortex and demonstrate better problem-solving and emotional regulation capacity.

3. **Perspective and circumstantial transformation:** Research in cognitive psychology demonstrates that cognitive reframing techniques can alter subjective experience without changing objective circumstances. Multiple studies show that individuals trained in perspective-shifting techniques report significantly higher life satisfaction and better stress resilience compared to control groups.

4. **Average as cultural failure concept:** Studies in social psychology show that cultures emphasizing exceptional achievement create higher rates of anxiety, depression, and perfectionism. Research indicates that societies promoting acceptance of "ordinary" success show better overall mental health outcomes and higher levels of community satisfaction.

5. **Ordinary actions and extraordinary outcomes:** Research in behavioral psychology demonstrates that consistent, small actions compound over time to create significant results.

Studies show that individuals focusing on daily consistency rather than dramatic interventions achieve substantially higher success rates in long-term goal achievement.

6. **Perspective distortion patterns:** Clinical research from the Beck Institute identifies three primary patterns of perspective distortion: catastrophizing, unrealistic optimism, and cognitive rigidity. Cognitive behavioral therapy research shows that interventions addressing these specific distortions improve psychological well-being and decision-making capacity.

7. **Unrealistic expectations and disappointment:** Research in motivational psychology demonstrates that unrealistic expectations about change timelines and effort requirements predict higher rates of goal abandonment and decreased motivation. Studies indicate that realistic expectation-setting significantly increases persistence in goal pursuit over extended periods.

8. **Productive versus destructive stress:** Research in stress physiology shows that acute stress enhances performance and builds resilience when followed by adequate recovery periods. Studies demonstrate that chronic stress without resolution creates measurable physiological damage and cognitive impairment through elevated cortisol and inflammatory responses.

9. **Present-moment awareness and anxiety reduction:** Mindfulness research demonstrates that present-moment focus activates the parasympathetic nervous system and reduces anxiety symptoms. Multiple studies show that individuals trained in present-moment awareness techniques show significant reductions in future-focused worry patterns and rumination.

10. **Stress capacity as trainable skill:** Research in resilience psychology demonstrates that stress resilience can be developed through graduated exposure and cognitive training. Studies show that individuals who practice stress reframing techniques develop measurable improvements in emotional regulation and stress response over time.

11. **Strengths-weaknesses paradox:** Research in personality psychology shows that personality traits exist on a continuum where strengths in excess become weaknesses and apparent weaknesses often contain adaptive advantages. Studies demonstrate that self-awareness of this paradox improves decision-making and reduces internal psychological conflict.

8: E – Edify
Heal Through Service

Among the many individuals I have had the opportunity to work with, one in particular stands out as one of the most hopeful people I ever had the pleasure of knowing. He was a youth coach who exemplified everything you hope to see in someone trusted to work with young people. Every athlete knew without question that this coach cared about them, and they knew that to him they were not just players, but he truly saw them as complete human beings navigating life's complexities.

Of course, he taught them the skills of the sport, but he went far beyond technique and strategy. He took time to talk with them about life choices that had nothing to do with athletics. He shed tears with them during their struggles and cheered with them in their victories. His impact extended far beyond any game or season because you could see that his ego wasn't involved. It was 100 percent about everyone else.

What made this coach even more remarkable was what you discovered about him outside the athletic realm. Professionally, he was wildly successful, owning multiple thriving businesses such as retail shops, restaurants, and more. Nonetheless, you would never know it from his behavior. He lived without pretension, finding meaning not in accumulation but in contribution. During our many conversations about life and priorities, I heard something that challenged my assumptions about wealth and success. Here was someone who could have anything he ever wanted simply by buying it, but he warned about how wealth can ruin families and it can be a curse if your heart isn't in the right place.

On top of his business responsibilities and coaching commitments, he somehow found time to serve the poor, constantly mentor others, and never hesitated to help others financially when the need arose. I am still in awe of how much he accomplished, but more importantly, how everything he did was in service of someone else.

As I was gathering the stories that would be included in this book, I found it interesting that this coach's example is different from the others in the prior chapters. I do not claim that I taught this coach anything. He's the one that taught me everything and added the final Pillar to my framework.

His example reminded me of something I remember from Mr. Rogers, the gentle TV personality many of us grew up with. When Mr. Rogers spoke about dealing with scary or overwhelming situations, he offered this wisdom: "Look for the helpers." In times of crisis or despair, he said, there are always people working to make things better. You might miss them, if you aren't looking for them. This coach was exactly that kind of helper. As children, it's comforting to look for the helpers in a scary world. Now that we're adults, the world doesn't just need us to look for the helpers. It needs us to become the helpers.

I see helpers everywhere, in every career and walk of life. They're the educators who sacrificed wealth because they knew they "wanted to make a difference." They're the grocery store clerks who genuinely care about their customers' day. They're the cafeteria workers who clean up spills without complaint. They're the strangers who offer their bus seats to young mothers. They're the people who choose respect over anger, even when they could easily justify making a scene because of someone else's mistake. These helpers don't seek attention or accolades. Instead, they seek to serve.

After working through the first five pillars of the WE HOPE framework, you might expect to feel completely restored. You've recognized your worth, protected your energy, built sustaining habits, seized opportunities, and shifted your perspective. These are significant accomplishments that create a foundation for lasting change.

However, something might still feel incomplete. You might notice that even with all this personal work, there's a restlessness that persists. You might have a sense that your healing journey, while meaningful, isn't quite finished. This feeling is actually pointing you toward the final piece of rebuilding hope.

The missing element is often connection to something larger than yourself. When you've been focused on personal healing and growth, it's natural to become somewhat inward-looking. This focus is necessary during the rebuilding process, but it becomes limiting if it continues indefinitely. True healing and lasting hope require moving beyond yourself to contribute to others.

The tricky thing about being in a rut is that you get so caught up in your own problems and issues that you don't have the energy or capacity to look outside yourself. The Pillar of Edify reminds you to clear those worn-out paths. You have to force yourself to get out of the house, turn off the streaming services, and step into the world. If you want to make a real difference in your life, you have to make a difference for someone else.

Notice that "edify" is the only pillar in the WE HOPE framework that is a verb—an action. Worth, energy, habits, opportunity, and perspective are all nouns that describe states of being or conditions you develop within yourself. Edify is fundamentally different because it requires you to focus entirely on outward action. This distinction is intentional and significant.

To edify means to build up, strengthen, or improve someone or something. In the context of hope, edification involves using your experiences, skills, and resources to contribute to the well-being of others. It's about taking what you've learned through your own struggles and using it to help others navigate theirs. The whole purpose of building hope is not just to feel better about your own life, but to take action that builds up others as well.

Hope that remains internal and self-focused eventually stagnates. Hope that flows outward through edification becomes a renewable resource that strengthens both you and those you serve. This is why, as we've seen throughout this framework, purpose serves as the foundation for every pillar—but nowhere is that purpose more clearly expressed than in the act of edifying others.

Edification isn't about grand gestures or dramatic acts of service. It's about recognizing that your healing becomes complete when it extends beyond yourself. The struggles you've faced, the growth you've experienced, and the hope you've rebuilt all become more meaningful when they're shared in service to others.

This chapter will explore how serving others becomes a pathway to deeper healing and more sustainable hope. You'll discover why connection and contribution are essential elements of psychological well-being, and you'll learn practical ways to build service into your routine without overwhelming yourself or neglecting your own needs. Most importantly, you'll learn how to do more than look for the helpers. You need to commit to being the helper the world desperately needs.

Why Serving Others Rebuilds Hope

The relationship between service and hope might not be immediately obvious, especially when you're still working on your own healing. It can seem counterintuitive to focus on others when you're still rebuilding your own foundation. However, research consistently shows that helping others creates psychological benefits that accelerate personal healing.[1]

Even the smallest act of service deepens your understanding and application of every other pillar in the WE HOPE framework. When you help others, you reinforce your sense of worth by seeing the tangible difference you make in their lives. Your inherent value becomes undeniable when you witness how your presence, skills, and care affect someone else positively. This external validation strengthens the internal worth you've been rebuilding.

Serving others also reveals how interconnected your energy management truly is. When you give of yourself in meaningful ways, you often discover that helping others actually energizes you rather than depletes you.[2] This paradox teaches you to distinguish between energy-giving and energy-draining activities in all areas of your life. You learn that protecting your energy isn't just about saying no but also about saying yes to the right things. Then, edifying others becomes a habit that reinforces all your other positive habits, creating opportunities that might never have appeared otherwise, while shifting your perspective from scarcity to abundance as you see how much you actually have to offer.

The act of helping others also activates what psychologists call the "helper's high."[3] This is a genuine physiological response that includes the release of endorphins and other neurotransmitters associated with well-being. The feeling isn't just emotional satisfaction but an actual chemical reward that your brain receives when you engage in prosocial behavior.

Service creates a sense of purpose that extends beyond personal achievement. When your actions directly improve someone else's life, you experience meaning that can't be replicated through self-focused activities.[4] This meaning becomes a source of motivation that sustains you through your own difficult moments. Even more powerful is when you intentionally serve others in a way that aligns with your purpose. Purpose-aligned service is one of the most powerful tools for a life ful of hope.

Serving others also helps you develop skills and perspectives that benefit your own life. When you help someone else solve a problem, you often gain insights that apply to your own challenges. When you offer encouragement to someone who's struggling, you practice the kind of self-compassion you need in your own life. The wisdom you share with others becomes wisdom you can access for yourself.

Serving others requires some authentic preparation and creativity. When I was a classroom teacher, I noticed a major shift in my ability to be effective when I started looking outward to plan each day. Once I started focusing on what the students needed to accomplish each day instead of my own checklist, the results were nothing short of life-altering. It seems like something so insignificant, but this slight shift from serving my needs to serving their needs made a tremendous impact on the environment of the class and the outcomes I intended. The students could tell that I was authentically there for them, and it encouraged them to be the best version of themselves that they could be.

The social connections that develop through service create a support network that enhances your own resilience.[5] When you show up for others consistently, they're more likely to show up for you when you need support. This mutual aid creates a safety net that reduces anxiety and increases hope.

Service also provides structure and routine that can be especially helpful during periods of personal instability. When you commit to helping others regularly, you create external accountability that gets you out of your own head and into action. This forward momentum often carries over into other areas of your life.

Perhaps most importantly, service reminds you that you have agency and influence in the world. When you're struggling with personal challenges, it's easy to feel powerless and ineffective. Helping others provides immediate evidence that you can make a positive difference.[6] This evidence rebuilds confidence in your ability to create change, both in your own life and in the world around you.

Losing Yourself to Find Yourself

The phrase "losing yourself to find yourself" might sound like a contradiction, but it captures an essential truth about human psychology and personal growth. When you're absorbed in your own problems and focused primarily on your own needs, you often lose sight of who you really are and what you're capable of becoming.

This self-focus isn't inherently wrong, and it's often necessary during periods of crisis or rebuilding. However, when it becomes the primary mode of operation, it can actually limit your growth and healing. You begin to see yourself only in relation to your problems rather than in relation to your potential contributions.

The paradox of Edify is that you must not expect anything from those you serve. Sure, you benefit exponentially when you serve others, but if you truly want to build those around you, you have to shed a lot of your own self inclinations towards feeling entitled to gain favor or to judge others. In short, you cannot serve others and your ego at the same time.

When you lose yourself in service to others, you discover aspects of your personality and capabilities that might remain hidden otherwise. You might discover that you're naturally good at listening, that you have a gift for encouragement, or that you're skilled at helping people see solutions to their problems. These discoveries expand your self-concept beyond your struggles and limitations.

Service also helps you experience what psychologists call "flow states" where you become completely absorbed in meaningful activity. During these states, self-consciousness disappears and you become fully engaged with the task at hand. These experiences provide relief from the self-focused rumination that often accompanies personal struggles.

Many times, I would get so involved in my classroom lessons and instruction, that I fully lost track of time. The students could tell I was excited, and I could tell that they were engaged. We would have deep, thoughtful conversations about literature, or life, or both. At the end of the lesson, I would hear comments about how quickly class had flown by, or that they wished they could stay and continue the discussion. Those moments are something that I will always cherish and strive to recapture as I seek to continue to edify myself and others. When I shifted my focus back to edifying my students, my employment shifted back from being a job to being so much more. At times, it even felt like a spiritual calling.

The temporary loss of self-focus that comes with service should never lead you to neglect your own needs or become codependent. Instead, you need to recognize that your identity is larger than your problems and that your purpose extends beyond your personal healing. This expanded sense of self creates more space for hope because it's not limited by your current circumstances.

When you're helping others, you often access strengths and resources you didn't know you had.[7] You might find courage you didn't think you possessed, wisdom you didn't realize you'd gained, or compassion you hadn't fully developed. These discoveries become part of your evolving self-concept and evidence of your continued growth.

Service also provides perspective on your own healing journey. When you see others facing similar struggles, you gain insight into your own patterns and progress. You might realize that you've come further than you thought, or you might discover new approaches to challenges you're still facing. This perspective accelerates your own healing while helping others with theirs.

The paradox of losing yourself to find yourself resolves when you understand that your true self is not separate from your relationships and contributions. You don't exist in isolation but as part of a larger web of connections and interdependence. When you honor this interconnectedness through service, you discover more of who you really are.

Building Edification Into Your Routine

Creating a sustainable practice of service requires intentionality and planning. Random acts of kindness are valuable, but they don't provide the consistent benefits that come from regular, committed service.[8] Building edification into your routine means finding ways to serve others that align with your schedule, energy level, and capabilities.

Start by identifying your natural strengths and interests. What do you enjoy doing? What comes easily to you? What skills have you developed through your own challenges and growth? How do these areas overlap with your purpose? These strengths become the foundation for your service activities. When you serve others using your natural gifts, the experience is energizing rather than draining.

You should also consider your available time and energy realistically. Service should enhance your life, not overwhelm it. If you're still in the early stages of rebuilding your own foundation, start with small commitments that don't strain your resources. A few hours per month might be more sustainable than a few hours per week.

Look for opportunities that align with your schedule and lifestyle. If you're a morning person, consider volunteering at breakfast programs or morning activities. If you have limited transportation, look for opportunities in your immediate neighborhood or that can be done remotely. If you have childcare responsibilities, look for family-friendly service opportunities.

Think about the causes or populations that resonate with your own experiences.[9] If you've struggled with mental health challenges, you might be drawn to supporting others facing similar issues. If you've overcome financial difficulties, you might want to help others develop financial literacy. Your personal experiences become assets that enhance your ability to serve effectively.

Consider both formal and informal opportunities for service. Formal volunteering with established organizations provides structure and training, but informal service to neighbors, friends, or community members can be equally meaningful. Both types of service contribute to your sense of purpose and connection.

Build service into your existing habits and routines rather than treating it as a separate activity. This might mean offering to help neighbors with groceries when you're already going to the store, or using your professional skills to help nonprofit organizations during your lunch breaks, or incorporating service projects into family activities.

Start with commitments you can maintain consistently rather than ambitious projects you might abandon.[10] Regular, small acts of service create more lasting benefits than sporadic, large gestures. Consistency builds relationships and trust that enhance the impact of your service.

Monitor your energy and motivation levels as you develop your service routine. Service should generally increase your energy and hope rather than deplete them. If you find that your service activities are adding stress or exhaustion, consider adjusting your approach or scale.

Remember that service can take many forms. Direct service to individuals, contributing to organizations, advocacy for causes, and even informal support to friends and family all count as edification. The key is finding approaches that feel meaningful to you, that are sustainable over time, and that allow you to see others be authentically grateful for your sacrifice on their behalf.

Service as Purpose in Action

Service transforms abstract concepts of purpose into concrete actions with visible impact. When you're struggling to find meaning in your life or wondering what your purpose might be, service provides a practical way to explore these questions through experimentation rather than just contemplation.

Many people feel paralyzed by the pressure to discover their "life purpose" as if it's a fixed destination they need to find. Service reveals that purpose is often discovered through action rather than analysis. When you begin serving others, you learn what energizes you, what skills you want to develop, and what kinds of impact feel most meaningful to you.

This is precisely what I witnessed in the coach whose story opened this chapter. His purpose wasn't something he discovered through soul-searching or career counseling, but it emerged through his consistent choice to serve young athletes. With every tearful conversation, every life lesson shared between drills, every act of quiet generosity, he was living his purpose in real time. His multiple successful businesses could have easily become his identity, but he understood that true fulfillment came from building up others.

Service also demonstrates that purpose doesn't have to be grand or unique to be valid. The person who helps elderly neighbors with technology problems is living their purpose just as much as the person who starts a nonprofit organization. Purpose is about aligning your actions with your values and using your capabilities to make a positive difference, regardless of the scale. Remember those everyday helpers we discussed—the grocery store clerk who genuinely cares, the cafeteria worker who cleans without complaint, the stranger who offers a seat on the bus. Each of these individuals is living their purpose through simple acts of service.

When educators tell me they became teachers because they "wanted to make a difference," they're describing what they thought was their original purpose. When they've lost hope in their careers, it's often because they've disconnected from that purpose, not because the purpose has disappeared. They might not recognize the ways that they are edifying others through their purpose or they might have lost touch with their purpose entirely. The Pillar of Edify calls them—calls all of us—back to that foundational why. It transforms the abstract desire to "make a difference" into specific, actionable ways to serve.

For me, sharing the ideas that I've compiled in this book is one way that I've chosen to implement the Pillar of Edify. I whole-heartedly believe in these concepts, and I know that I am living my purpose when I am bringing hope into the life of someone who is seeing that spark slowly fade. I've been there and know how much these Pillars saved me. I never intended to become an author, nor do I have a desire to evangelize my work, but I couldn't keep this work to myself any longer. Like that coach who couldn't help but pour into every athlete he encountered, I found that my healing became complete only when it flowed outward to others.

Through service, you discover that your purpose might be different from what you expected. You might think you want to help people through counseling, but discover that you're more energized by helping them develop practical skills. You might think you're drawn to working with children, but find that you're more effective with adults. Service provides real-world testing of your assumptions about your interests and gifts.

Service also reveals that purpose can evolve and expand over time.[11] As you grow and develop new capabilities, your service can grow and develop as well. What starts as informal help to neighbors might evolve into formal volunteer leadership. What begins as personal healing might expand into helping others with similar challenges.

The immediate feedback you receive through service helps you understand the impact of your actions in ways that many careers don't provide. When you help someone learn a new skill, comfort someone in distress, or contribute to a cause you care about, you see direct evidence of your influence. This feedback loop reinforces your sense of purpose and motivates continued growth. This is why that coach's happiness was so evident. He could see daily how his investment in young people was shaping their character and choices.

Service connects your personal healing journey to something larger than yourself. The struggles you've faced and the growth you've experienced become resources for helping others rather than just personal achievements. This connection creates meaning that extends beyond individual success to collective well-being.

Your service also becomes a way of living your values rather than just holding them as beliefs. If you value compassion, service provides opportunities to practice compassion. If you value justice, service provides ways to work toward justice. If you value growth, service provides contexts for continued growth, learning, and development.

The Pillar of Edify demonstrates that purpose doesn't require perfection or complete healing before you can contribute. Your ongoing struggles and imperfections don't disqualify you from helping others. They often become sources of authenticity and connection that enhance your ability to serve effectively. Now, all that is left is your commitment to go and be the helper that the world needs you to be.

Stone Upon Stone—Building Your Pillar

Base

Service and Connection Assessment:

Complete this research-based assessment to understand how your current perspective may be supporting or hindering your hope. For each statement, rate yourself on a scale of 1-5 (1 = never true, 5 = always

1. I regularly notice opportunities to help others in small ways throughout my day
2. When I help someone else, I feel energized rather than drained
3. I can see how my personal struggles have given me insights that could help others
4. I believe I have valuable skills or experiences to offer, even if they seem ordinary
5. I feel comfortable receiving gratitude without deflecting or minimizing my contribution
6. I can serve others without expecting recognition or reciprocation
7. I naturally look for ways to build others up rather than compete with them
8. I feel a sense of purpose when my actions positively impact someone else
9. I can balance taking care of my own needs while also caring for others
10. I believe that helping others is essential to my own healing and growth

Reflection Questions:

After completing the assessment, reflect on these questions:
- Which statements scored lowest for you? What patterns do you notice about your relationship with service?
- Think about the last time you helped someone and felt genuinely fulfilled by the experience (not obligated or resentful). What was different about that situation?
- Complete this sentence honestly: "I would be more willing to serve others if I could stop believing that _____."
- When you consider "losing yourself to find yourself," what fears or resistance come up? What do you worry you might lose?

Service Strengths Inventory:

Reflect on your personal experiences and identify your potential service strengths:

- ° What challenges have you overcome that others might be facing now?
- ° What skills do you have that feel natural or come easily to you?
- ° When others come to you for help or advice, what do they usually seek?
- ° What activities make you feel most energized and engaged?
- ° How might these strengths align with your purpose statement from Chapter 2?

Write down 3-5 specific ways your experiences and strengths could benefit others.

Column

Service Integration Challenge:
This challenge will help you build sustainable service habits that align with your natural strengths and available resources.

Days 1-3: Micro-Service Awareness Each day, complete three "micro-services"—small acts of service that take less than 5 minutes each:

- ° Hold a door, offer a genuine compliment, listen fully to someone who needs to talk
- ° Help a coworker with a simple task, text encouragement to a friend, let someone go ahead of you in line
- ° Share useful information, pick up litter, express genuine gratitude to someone who serves you

Document each micro-service and notice:

- ° How did you feel before, during, and after each act?
- ° What was the other person's response?
- ° Which acts felt most natural to you?

Days 4-6: Strength-Based Service Using your Service Strengths Inventory from the Base exercise, identify one strength-based service opportunity each day:

- ° If you're good at listening, offer to be a sounding board for someone facing a decision
- ° If you have organizational skills, help someone declutter or plan something
- ° If you have knowledge in a specific area, offer to teach or mentor someone
- ° If you're good at encouragement, check in with someone who's struggling

For each strength-based service:

- ° Choose actions that align with your current capacity (don't overwhelm yourself)
- ° Focus on being genuinely helpful rather than impressive

° Notice how using your natural strengths in service feels different from obligatory helping

Days 7-10: Purpose-Aligned Service Design Create a simple, sustainable service routine that connects to your purpose statement:
   ° Identify one recurring service opportunity that you can commit to (weekly, bi-weekly, or monthly)
   ° This could be formal volunteering, informal community help, or regular support to specific individuals
   ° The commitment should feel manageable and energizing, not burdensome
   ° Take your first action toward this commitment (research organizations, reach out to someone, or start the activity)

Daily Documentation: Each evening, spend 5 minutes writing:
   ° How did serving others today affect my own sense of hope and energy?
   ° What did I notice about my capacity to "lose myself" in service to others?
   ° When did I feel most authentically helpful versus when did I feel like I was performing?
   ° What resistance or unexpected emotions came up around serving others?

End-of-Challenge Integration: After 10 days, reflect on:
   ° Which type of service felt most sustainable and energizing?
   ° How has your perspective on your own healing journey changed through serving others?
   ° What evidence did you gather that you have valuable contributions to make?
   ° What sustainable service practice will you continue moving forward?
   ° How has serving others strengthened the other pillars of your WE HOPE framework?

Capstone

Books:
   The Second Mountain by David Brooks
   Give and Take by Adam Grant
   The Power of Giving by Azim Jamal
   Bowling Alone by Robert Putnam
Podcasts:
   Hidden Brain: "The Psychology of Self-Sacrifice"

The Science of Happiness: "How Helping Others Helps You"

On Being: "The Spiritual Practice of Service"

WorkLife: "The Science of Generosity"

Articles:

"Helper's High: The Science Behind the Joy of Giving" (Psychology Today)

"The Benefits of Volunteering for Personal Growth" (Journal of Community Psychology)

"Service Learning and Mental Health Outcomes" (American Journal of Community Psychology)

"Can Altruism Help Us Through Hard Times?" (Greater Good Science Center)

Chapter Notes:

1. **Altruism and personal healing acceleration:** Studies from the University of California, San Francisco show that individuals engaged in regular volunteer activities demonstrate faster recovery from depression and trauma. Research indicates that helping others activates the brain's reward centers while simultaneously reducing activity in stress-related neural networks, creating measurable improvements in mental health within 8-12 weeks of consistent service.

2. **Paradoxical energizing effects of service:** Multiple studies demonstrate that meaningful service activities can increase rather than decrease personal energy levels in most participants. Research indicates that purpose-driven helping behaviors may activate the parasympathetic nervous system and increase oxytocin production.

3. **Helper's high neurological research:** Neuroscience research confirms that acts of kindness trigger the release of endorphins, serotonin, and dopamine while reducing cortisol levels. The "helper's high" creates measurable brain chemistry changes that appear to last longer than satisfaction from self-focused activities.

4. **Service-derived meaning versus achievement-based satisfaction:** Research demonstrates that meaning derived from helping others creates more sustained psychological well-being than meaning derived from personal accomplishment. Studies indicate that service-based purpose shows greater stability over time compared to achievement-based purpose during life transitions and setbacks.

5. **Reciprocal support networks through service:** Studies show that individuals who engage in regular service develop stronger social support networks, with volunteers reporting more people they could rely on during crises. Research demonstrates that service creates bidirectional relationships where helpers receive emotional and practical support from those they serve and their service communities.

6. **Service and personal agency restoration:** Research from the University of Pennsylvania demonstrates that helping others measurably increases perceived personal control and self-efficacy. Studies show that individuals recovering from trauma or depression who engage in service report greater confidence in their ability to influence positive outcomes in their own lives.

7. **Hidden strengths discovery through service:** Studies from the University of Washington show that most volunteers discover previously unknown personal strengths through service activities. Research indicates that helping others provides unique contexts for accessing capabilities that don't emerge in typical work or personal settings, leading to expanded self-awareness and confidence.

8. **Consistency versus intensity in service benefits:** Studies show that regular, small acts of service create more lasting psychological benefits than infrequent, large service commitments. Research demonstrates that weekly service activities produce greater improvements in mood, purpose, and social connection compared to monthly intensive service projects.

9. **Experiential alignment in effective service:** Individuals who serve populations or causes connected to their personal experiences show higher satisfaction and effectiveness rates. Studies indicate that experiential alignment creates authentic empathy and practical wisdom that enhances both the helper's growth and the quality of service provided.

10. **Sustainable service commitment patterns:** Studies in positive psychology show that volunteers who start with small, manageable commitments are more likely to maintain service activities long-term. Research indicates that gradual service expansion creates sustainable habits while preventing burnout and overcommitment that often leads to service abandonment.

11. **Purpose evolution and adaptation:** Research from the University of Southern California demonstrates that purpose naturally evolves as individuals develop new capabilities and life experiences.

Part 3

Beyond The Pinnacle

9: Everyday Hope
Pillars of Hope—Pillars of Life

You've worked through the six pillars of the WE HOPE framework. You've recognized your inherent worth, learned to protect your energy, built sustainable habits, trained yourself to see opportunities, shifted your perspective, and discovered the healing power of service. These aren't just concepts anymore but practices you've integrated into your life. The question now becomes: what does it actually look like to live with hope on a daily basis?

The transition from learning about hope to living with hope happens in what we might call the "messy middle"—that space between understanding principles and trusting yourself to apply them imperfectly in real situations.[1] It's where the neat categories you've studied collide with the complexity of actual life, and you discover that hope is about staying engaged with the process.

Consider the new parent who memorized every sleep training method, only to find their child doesn't respond to any of them. Living with hope means adapting what they learned, trusting their instincts, and finding peace with the reality that some nights will simply be harder than others. The hope isn't in the perfect execution of technique but in their willingness to keep showing up with love.

Another example could be the person who learned all the networking strategies for career advancement, then finds themselves tongue-tied at their first professional event. Living with hope means having a genuine conversation with one person instead of working the entire room, recognizing that authentic connection matters more than perfect execution of learned tactics.

Living with hope could be the individual who studied meditation and mindfulness practices, then faced their first major crisis since beginning their practice. Living with hope means noticing their anxiety without judging themselves for not being "zen enough," using whatever tools work in the moment, and recognizing that growth includes setbacks.

You might think about the community volunteer who learned about improving their community through social engagement, then shows up to their first neighborhood meeting where long-time residents resist their ideas for change. It might be difficult at first, but living with hope means listening more than speaking, building relationships before pushing agendas, and finding common ground they never learned about in their books.

The transition from learning about hope to living with hope can feel uncertain. You might wonder if you're doing it right or if the changes you've made will last. You might worry that without the structure of working through each pillar systematically, you'll lose momentum or fall back into old patterns. These concerns are natural and understandable. They are signs that you're in the midst of the messy middle, where the real growth happens.

Living with hope doesn't mean you'll never struggle again or that every day will feel bright and optimistic. Hope isn't a permanent emotional state but a way of approaching life that remains available to you even during difficult seasons.[2] It's a skill set you can access when you need it and a perspective you can return to when you've temporarily lost your way.

This chapter explores what everyday hope looks like in practice. You'll discover how to integrate the framework into your regular routines without it feeling forced or artificial. You'll learn to recognize the signs of a hopeful life and understand that hope expresses itself differently in different contexts and seasons.

Putting the Framework Together

The WE HOPE framework isn't meant to be followed in a rigid, linear sequence once you've learned it. While working through each pillar systematically is helpful during the initial learning phase, everyday application is much more fluid and intuitive, where principles meet real life with all its unpredictability.[3] You'll find yourself drawing on different pillars at different times based on what life presents to you, often discovering that your intuitive response combines several pillars in ways you never planned.

When constructing the ancient Greek temples, the builders didn't put up the first pillar and then start building the pediment on top of that first support. Instead, each pillar had to be built simultaneously. Once each column was solidly in place, work could begin on the upper structures, finalized with the addition of the beautiful and dramatic friezes. These decorative bands immortalized the stories of ancient heroes. Similarly, by applying the WE HOPE framework, this phase of consistently living with hope will help you transcend the mediocre and live on an elevated plane. Maybe one day, people will look to your story and your example for inspiration and guidance.

Picture Sarah, rushing through her morning routine when she discovers her coffee maker has broken. In the learning phase, she might have tried to identify which pillar applies here. In the messy middle of living hope, she automatically draws on energy management (choosing tea instead of stressing about the coffee shop line), perspective (recognizing this isn't catastrophic), and opportunity (texting her neighbor to ask about borrowing a cup, strengthening their relationship). She's not thinking about the framework—she's living it.

Some days you might wake up feeling energized and clear about your worth, naturally gravitating toward opportunity and service. Other days you might need to focus primarily on basic habits and energy management just to get through. Both approaches represent hope in action because you're responding to your actual needs rather than forcing yourself into a predetermined pattern.

The interconnected nature of the pillars becomes more apparent as you live with them over time. Working on your habits naturally supports your energy management. Practicing service reinforces your sense of worth. Maintaining perspective helps you recognize opportunities. These connections create a reinforcing cycle that makes hope increasingly sustainable.[4]

You'll also discover that different life circumstances call for emphasis on different pillars. During periods of high stress, you might focus more heavily on energy protection and perspective. During times of transition, opportunity recognition and habit building might take precedence. During relationship challenges, service and worth might be most relevant. This flexibility is a strength of the framework, not a weakness.

Take Elena, navigating a particularly challenging week when her elderly mother is hospitalized while she's facing a work deadline. In the learning phase, she might have felt overwhelmed trying to apply all six pillars equally. Living in the messy middle, she intuitively emphasizes the pillars that serve her most: energy management (asking her sister to take the evening hospital shift so she can sleep), perspective (reminding herself that both crises are temporary), and service (bringing coffee to the nursing staff who are caring for her mother). She's not neglecting the other pillars, but she just keeps them operating quietly in the background while three take center stage.

It would be impossible to perfectly balance your life across all six pillars at all times. However, you can develop the wisdom to know which pillar needs attention in any given moment and the skill to apply that pillar effectively. Sometimes hope means pushing yourself toward growth and opportunity. Sometimes hope means protecting your energy and focusing on basic self-care. Both responses can be equally valid expressions of hope.

Additionally, applying the framework might look slightly different depending upon situational contexts. For example, the Pillars that need to be applied in your family life might look different that what you are experiencing at work. The Pillars for an entrepreneur might be applied differently that someone who is a teacher, a nurse, a lawyer, or any other profession. With that in mind, don't forget to explore the WE HOPE guides. You might find some practical applications for your situation. If you happen to see a place where WE HOPE applies, and there isn't a guide, send us a proposal. We are constantly looking for opportunities to update.

As you continue practicing, you'll develop intuitive awareness of which pillar needs attention. You might notice that feeling overwhelmed often signals a need for better energy management. Feeling stuck might indicate it's time to focus on opportunity or perspective. Feeling isolated might suggest the need for more service or connection. These internal signals become a guidance system for applying the framework.

Remember that mastery doesn't mean perfection. You'll still have days when you forget to apply what you've learned or when you slip back into old patterns. You'll have mornings when you choose scrolling your phone over your morning routine, afternoons when you snap at a colleague despite knowing better, evenings when you isolate instead of reaching out for connection. These lapses don't represent failure but normal parts of the learning process.

The difference is that now you have tools to recognize what's happening and strategies to get back on track more quickly.

What Does the Hopeful Person Do?

The hopeful person doesn't live in constant optimism or maintain unwavering confidence about the future. Instead, they've developed a set of practices and perspectives that help them navigate uncertainty with resilience and purpose. Understanding what hope looks like in daily life helps you recognize it in yourself and continue developing it.

Hopeful people have learned to sit with discomfort without immediately trying to escape it.[5] They don't avoid difficult emotions or challenging situations, but they also don't get trapped by them. They've developed the ability to experience struggle while maintaining belief in their capacity to work through it. This emotional resilience isn't about being tough or stoic but about trusting the process of growth and healing.

The hopeful person maintains routines and habits that support their well-being even when they don't feel like it.[6] They understand that motivation isn't required for action and that consistency in small things creates stability for handling larger challenges. Their daily practices aren't rigid or joyless but provide structure that enables flexibility in other areas.

Hopeful people actively look for opportunities rather than waiting for good things to happen to them. They've trained themselves to notice possibilities that others might miss because they're not focused on what's wrong or lacking. This doesn't mean they ignore problems or challenges but that they maintain awareness of potential solutions and positive developments.

The hopeful person has learned to manage their perspective consciously. They recognize when they're catastrophizing or getting stuck in negative thought patterns and have strategies for shifting their focus. They practice gratitude not as a forced positivity exercise but as a way of training their attention toward what's working in their lives.

Hopeful people understand the value of service and connection.[7] They've discovered that contributing to others' well-being enhances their own sense of purpose and resilience. Their service isn't motivated by obligation or guilt but by genuine understanding that individual healing connects to collective healing.

The hopeful person doesn't pretend that their struggles don't exist or that positive thinking alone will solve their problems. They've learned to hold both difficulty and possibility simultaneously. They can acknowledge what's hard while maintaining belief in their ability to create positive change.

Hopeful people have developed realistic expectations about growth and change. They understand that progress isn't always linear and that setbacks don't negate their overall development. They've learned to measure success by their response to challenges rather than by the absence of challenges.

The hopeful person practices self-compassion when they make mistakes or fall short of their goals.[8] They treat themselves with the same kindness they would offer a good friend facing similar struggles. This self-compassion becomes a source of resilience that enables them to keep trying even after failures.

Hopeful people maintain connection to their values and purpose even when external circumstances are difficult. They've learned to find meaning in their response to situations they can't control. Their sense of purpose isn't dependent on everything going well but on their commitment to living according to their principles.

As you practice these skills, you will begin to recognize attributes in yourself and others that embody hope. How do you know when hope is becoming your natural response rather than something you have to work at? The signs are often subtle but unmistakable once you learn to recognize them:

You show **resilience without rigidity** when you bounce back from setbacks more quickly, but you're not afraid to feel the full weight of disappointment first. You've learned that hope isn't about avoiding pain but about trusting your ability to move through it.

When faced with challenges, your first instinct becomes "What can I learn from this?" rather than "Why is this happening to me?" You experience **curiosity over certainty** when you find yourself genuinely interested in solutions rather than fixated on problems.

You notice **natural service tendencies** in yourself by helping others without calculation or expectation. Holding the door, listening to a colleague's struggle, or picking up litter becomes automatic—not because you should, but because connection feels natural.

You demonstrate **energy awareness** because you've become attuned to what drains and energizes you. You start making small adjustments throughout the day by choosing different routes, sitting in different locations, and having conversations that feed rather than deplete you.

You catch yourself spiraling less often because of your **perspective flexibility**, and when you do spiral, you can shift more quickly.[9] You develop what we might call "meta-hope"—hope about your ability to find hope even when you've temporarily lost it.

Hope isn't a static state but a dynamic response that adapts to life's changing circumstances. Understanding how hope expresses itself across different seasons helps you recognize it even when it doesn't look like what you expected. Hope might look like basic survival skills such as maintaining sleep schedules, asking for help, focusing on today rather than tomorrow. Hope becomes about embracing uncertainty rather than controlling outcomes. When life is expanding with new opportunities, relationships, or achievements, hope means staying connected to your values rather than getting swept away by momentum. It's about integrating success without losing sight of what truly matters.

During stable periods when nothing dramatic is happening, hope means finding meaning in ordinary moments. It's appreciating the luxury of boredom, investing in relationships that don't need you, and preparing for seasons of challenge that will inevitably come.

Finding Hope in Everyday Situations

Hope expresses itself differently in various contexts and relationships. Understanding how to apply the Pillars of Hope in specific areas of life helps you integrate the framework more naturally into your daily experience. The key is learning to recognize hope in ordinary situations rather than waiting for dramatic moments of transformation.

Work

In your professional life, hope might mean approaching challenges as opportunities for growth rather than threats to your security. The hopeful employee doesn't avoid difficult projects but sees them as chances to develop new skills and demonstrate capabilities. They maintain perspective about workplace conflicts, recognizing that disagreements can lead to better solutions when handled constructively.

Hope at work involves managing your energy throughout the day rather than pushing through exhaustion. The hopeful worker takes breaks when needed, sets boundaries around overtime, and finds ways to align their daily tasks with their larger sense of purpose. They understand that sustainable performance requires attention to their well-being.

The hopeful person seeks opportunities to contribute beyond their basic job requirements. They might mentor newer employees, volunteer for projects that interest them, or suggest improvements to existing processes. This service orientation enhances their sense of meaning and often leads to unexpected opportunities for advancement.

Hope in the workplace includes maintaining perspective about setbacks and disappointments. The hopeful employee doesn't interpret constructive feedback as personal attack or assume that one mistake defines their entire performance. They learn from failures and maintain belief in their ability to improve and succeed.

Family

Within family relationships, hope means maintaining connection and love even during periods of conflict or disagreement. The hopeful family member doesn't write off relationships because of past hurts but works toward healing and understanding. They recognize that family dynamics can change and that their own growth can positively influence the entire system.

Hope in family life involves modeling the principles you're learning rather than trying to change or fix other family members. The hopeful person focuses on their own behavior and responses while maintaining appropriate boundaries with family members who might not be ready for change.

The hopeful family member practices service within their household, contributing to the well-being of others without keeping score or expecting immediate reciprocation. They understand that small acts of kindness and support create positive momentum that benefits everyone.

Hope in family relationships includes maintaining perspective about generational patterns and inherited challenges. The hopeful person recognizes that they can break negative cycles without blaming previous generations or expecting perfection from themselves.

Recreation

In recreational activities, hope means choosing pursuits that genuinely energize and fulfill you rather than just providing distraction from problems. The hopeful person uses leisure time intentionally, selecting activities that align with their values and contribute to their overall well-being.

Hope in recreation involves trying new activities and experiences even when you're not sure you'll be good at them. The hopeful person maintains a growth mindset about their capabilities and sees learning as enjoyable rather than threatening. They understand that the process of trying new things is valuable regardless of the outcome.

The hopeful person uses recreational time to build connections with others who share their interests. They join clubs, take classes, or participate in community activities that provide opportunities for meaningful relationships. They understand that social connection is essential for sustained well-being.

Service

In service activities, hope means approaching volunteer work or community involvement as opportunities for mutual benefit rather than one-way giving. The hopeful volunteer recognizes that they receive as much as they give through service and maintains realistic expectations about the impact they can have.

Hope in service involves choosing opportunities that align with your interests and capabilities rather than feeling obligated to help in ways that drain your energy. The hopeful person understands that sustainable service requires attention to their own needs and limitations.

The hopeful person uses service as a way of practicing and developing the skills they want to strengthen in other areas of life. They might volunteer in leadership roles to develop confidence, work with populations that challenge their assumptions, or contribute skills they want to improve.

Integrating Hope Into Your Routine

The journey from understanding hope to embodying it happens gradually, often imperceptibly.[10] You don't wake up one morning suddenly transformed into a "hopeful person." Instead, hope becomes woven into the fabric of your daily existence through small, consistent choices that accumulate over time.

The most sustainable way to live hopefully is to embed the WE HOPE framework into routines you already have rather than creating entirely new structures. Hope doesn't require dramatic lifestyle changes—it requires intentional awareness within your existing life. I am providing a few examples in the following sections, but you have many other ways to apply these principles, so don't assume that you are limited by what I offer.

Morning Integration

The morning pause doesn't require meditation or journaling or any specific ritual. It simply requires a moment of consciousness before automatically reaching for external stimulation. This could happen while brushing your teeth, making coffee, or even sitting in your car before starting it. The key is consistency in creating this small space of awareness, allowing the framework to guide your choices naturally.

Think about Marcus, a busy father of three who felt overwhelmed by the idea of adding another practice to his already packed schedule. Instead of trying to create a perfect morning routine, he started with one simple shift: before checking his phone each morning, he would pause and ask himself, "What does my energy need today?" This single question naturally drew from multiple pillars (energy management, habits, and opportunity recognition) without feeling forced or artificial.

Some mornings, his energy needed protection, so he would skip reading news headlines that typically stressed him out. Other mornings, his energy felt abundant, so he might choose to walk to work instead of driving, creating an opportunity for exercise and reflection. The question became a gateway that connected him to his inner wisdom about what would serve him best that day.

Workday Integration

Sarah realized that her lunch break had become a mindless routine of scrolling social media while eating at her desk. She started practicing what she called the "possibility scan" which meant spending two minutes of her lunch break noticing one opportunity for growth, connection, or service in her afternoon. Her goal was to train her attention to see openings that already existed but often went unnoticed.

On challenging days, her possibility scan might reveal an opportunity to practice patience with a difficult colleague. On routine days, she might notice a chance to mentor a newer team member or suggest an improvement to a process. On days when her work felt meaningless, she might recognize an opportunity to find purpose in how she treated the custodial staff or responded to customer service calls. The practice gradually shifted her default perspective from "getting through the day" to "engaging with the day."

During your lunch break, instead of scrolling social media, practice the "possibility scan." The possibility scan works because it doesn't require you to change your circumstances. You only need to change your attention. It acknowledges that every day contains opportunities that we miss when we're focused solely on problems or routine tasks. This practice can happen during any transitional moment like walking to a meeting, waiting for an elevator, or sitting in traffic.

Evening Integration

Evening integration often proves most challenging because end-of-day energy is typically depleted. Traditional reflection practices can feel like additional work rather than restoration. Instead of reviewing everything that went wrong or creating elaborate gratitude lists, try a simple "pillar check-in" where you notice which pillar served you most today and which might need attention tomorrow.

James found that his evenings had become a cycle of rehashing work frustrations with his partner, creating stress for both of them. His pillar check-in revealed patterns he hadn't noticed. On days when he neglected energy management by skipping lunch, he consistently struggled with perspective by evening. On days when he found small ways to serve others by helping a colleague with a project or mentoring a junior team member, he naturally felt more resilient when facing his own challenges.

This practice becomes a gentle way of learning from your day without harsh self-judgment. You might notice that strong habit days create more opportunities for service. You might discover that perspective challenges often signal a need for energy protection. These insights become guidance for tomorrow's choices rather than criticism of today's performance.

The key principle underlying all these integrations is consistency over intensity. Five minutes of conscious hope practice daily creates more lasting change than hour-long sessions once a week. The practices work because they meet you where you already are rather than requiring you to become someone different. They transform ordinary moments into opportunities for growth without adding overwhelming new commitments to your schedule.

The Paradox of Effortless Effort

The goal of integrating hope isn't to eliminate struggle but to struggle more skillfully. As the framework becomes natural, you'll notice something paradoxical: the more effortlessly you live hopefully, the more effort you're actually putting in—but it's effort aligned with your values rather than effort fighting against your nature.

You'll find yourself naturally gravitating toward people, places, and activities that support hope while naturally moving away from what undermines it. The shift happens gradually, often without conscious awareness.

You might find that conversations naturally become deeper because you're listening for what matters to people rather than waiting for your turn to speak. You might discover that you seek out challenges because you've learned to trust your ability to grow through difficulty. You might notice that you spontaneously help others because service has become a natural expression of your own well-being rather than an obligation.

This effortless effort extends to how you handle setbacks. Instead of berating yourself for mistakes or struggling against circumstances you can't control, you'll find yourself asking different questions: "What is this situation here to teach me?" "How can I use this challenge to strengthen the pillars I've been neglecting?" "What would it look like to respond to this setback in a way that increases rather than decreases hope?

The ancient Greek temples weren't beautiful because they avoided weathering. They were beautiful because they were built to weather storms with grace. Similarly, a hopeful life isn't one without difficulties but one structured to handle difficulties with resilience, meaning, and connection.

Hope isn't something you achieve and then maintain. It's something you practice and then receive. Each day offers fresh opportunities to choose hope over cynicism, connection over isolation, possibility over limitation. The framework gives you tools, but life gives you practice opportunities.

This is the paradox: the more you align with hope, the more you're able to handle difficulty without being destroyed by it. You develop the capacity to not just survive challenges but to grow stronger through them. Your struggles become skill-building opportunities rather than evidence of your inadequacy.

As you continue this journey, remember that becoming a person who lives hopefully is itself a service to the world. Your hope gives others permission to hope. Your resilience creates space for others to be vulnerable. Your willingness to keep growing in the midst of imperfection models what's possible for everyone around you.

The messy middle never really ends, but it does become more familiar, more manageable, and ultimately, more beautiful. Hope lives there, in the space between what is and what could be, sustained by your willingness to keep showing up with open hands and an open heart.

Stone Upon Stone—Building Your Pillar

Base

Everyday Hope Assessment:

Complete this research-based assessment to understand how your current perspective may be supporting or hindering your hope. For each statement, rate yourself on a scale of 1-5 (1 = never true, 5 = always

1. I naturally draw on different pillars of the framework based on what life presents to me
2. I can recognize which pillar needs attention in any given moment
3. I maintain hope-supporting routines even when I don't feel motivated
4. I bounce back from setbacks more quickly than I used to
5. I look for learning opportunities rather than dwelling on problems
6. I help others naturally without calculation or expectation
7. I make energy-aware choices throughout my day
8. I can shift my perspective when I catch myself spiraling
9. I find meaning in ordinary moments and stable periods
10. I trust my ability to navigate the "messy middle" of growth

Reflection Questions:

After completing the assessment, reflect on these questions:

- Which statements scored lowest for you? What patterns do you notice about your everyday hope practice?
- Think about a recent challenge where you successfully applied the framework without consciously thinking about it. What Pillars did you naturally draw upon?
- Complete this sentence honestly: "I struggle most with living hopefully when _____."
- Recall Sarah's broken coffee maker example from the chapter. Describe a similar moment when you could have responded with automatic hope but didn't. How might you respond differently now?

Framework Integration Inventory:

Review each Pillar and honestly assess where you stand:

- ° **Worth:** How consistently do I treat myself with inherent value regardless of performance?
- ° **Energy:** How aware am I of what drains and energizes me throughout the day?
- ° **Habits:** How reliable am I to myself in maintaining hope-supporting routines?
- ° **Opportunity:** How naturally do I notice possibilities rather than fixating on problems?
- ° **Perspective:** How quickly can I shift from catastrophizing to curious problem-solving?
- ° **Edify:** How often do I help others as a natural expression of my well-being?

Write down 2-3 sentences about your current relationship with each pillar.

Column

The Messy Middle Challenge:

This challenge will help you practice living with hope through the unpredictable realities of daily life.

Days 1-3: Intuitive Pillar Practice

Each morning, before checking your phone or diving into your routine, take 30 seconds to ask: "What does my hope need today?" Don't overthink it—trust your first instinct about which Pillar(s) to emphasize.

Examples:

- ° When I wake up feeling scattered, I will focus on energy management and habits
- ° When I wake up anxious about the future, I will emphasize perspective and opportunity
- ° When I wake up feeling isolated, I will prioritize service and worth

Document which Pillars you emphasized each day.

Days 4-6: Ordinary Moment Integration

Practice finding hope in three ordinary situations each day. Use the examples from the chapter as inspiration:

- ° **Work Moments:** Approach one routine task with curiosity instead of just getting through it

- **Family Interactions:** Respond to conflict or stress with one pillar-informed choice
- **Recreation Time:** Choose activities that genuinely energize rather than just distract
- **Service Opportunities:** Notice one small way to contribute without being asked

For each ordinary moment, write:
- What happened?
- Which Pillars guided your response?
- How did this feel different from your typical approach?

Days 7-10: Effortless Effort Practice
Focus on the paradox described in the chapter—putting in effort that aligns with your values rather than fighting against your nature. Each day, identify one area where you've been struggling or forcing outcomes:
- A relationship where you're trying too hard to fix or change someone
- A work situation where you're pushing against circumstances you can't control
- A personal goal where you're being harshly self-critical
- A habit you're trying to build through willpower alone

Practice "effortless effort" by:
- Accepting what you cannot control in this situation
- Identifying what you can control (usually your response)
- Choosing one hope-aligned action that feels sustainable rather than forced
- Trusting the process rather than demanding specific outcomes

Daily Documentation: Each evening, spend 5 minutes writing:
- Which pillars did I draw on today, and how did they support each other?
- When did I feel most aligned with hope? Most resistant to it?
- What did I notice about the difference between forced effort and effortless effort?
- How is my response to challenges changing through this practice?

End-of-Challenge Integration: After 10 days, reflect on:
- Which pillar combinations felt most natural to you?
- How has your relationship with the "messy middle" of growth evolved?
- What evidence do you have that hope is becoming a more natural response?
- What sustainable integration practices will you continue?
- How might your example of living hopefully serve others around you?

Capstone

Books:

The Happiness Advantage by Shawn Anchor

Flourish by Martin Seligman

The How of Happiness by Sonja Lyubomirsky

Designing Your Life by Burnett and Evans

Podcasts:

The Happiness Lab with Dr Laurie Santos

Unlocking Us: "The Hard Parts of Hope"

The Life Coach School Podcast with Brooke Castillo

Optimal Living Daily

Articles:

"The Science of Well-Being" (Yale University Course Materials)

"Daily Practices for Sustainable Happiness" (Journal of Positive Psychology)

"The Role of Hope in Daily Stress Management" (Applied Psychology Research)

"Integrating Positive Psychology into Everyday Life" (Harvard Health Publishing)

Chapter Notes:

1. **Messy middle psychology:** Research in developmental psychology demonstrates that the transition from knowledge acquisition to practical application involves what researchers call "productive struggle." Studies from the University of Rochester show that individuals who expect and accept this transitional difficulty demonstrate higher rates of long-term skill integration compared to those who expect linear progress.

2. **Hope as dynamic skill versus emotional state**: Longitudinal studies from the University of Kansas demonstrate that hope functions as a cognitive skill set rather than a fixed emotional state. Research shows that individuals who understand hope as learnable and situational maintain higher resilience during difficult periods compared to those who view hope as dependent on external circumstances.

3. **Flexible framework application:** Research in implementation science shows that rigid adherence to behavioral frameworks produces lower success rates than flexible, context-sensitive application. Studies demonstrate that individuals who adapt evidence-based principles to their specific circumstances achieve better long-term outcomes.

4. **Interconnected skill development:** Research in systems psychology shows that personal development skills create reinforcing cycles where progress in one area enhances capacity in related areas. Studies indicate that interventions addressing multiple interconnected factors simultaneously produce better outcomes than single-focus approaches.

5. **Distress tolerance:** Clinical research from the University of Washington shows that distress tolerance is a learnable skill that significantly predicts resilience during challenging circumstances. Studies in dialectical behavior therapy demonstrate that individuals who practice sitting with discomfort without immediate action show reduced anxiety and improved emotional regulation.

6. **Self-compassion and resilience:** Extensive research by Dr. Kristin Neff demonstrates that self-compassion significantly predicts resilience, motivation, and psychological well-being. Studies show that individuals who practice self-kindness maintain higher motivation after failures and demonstrate better long-term goal achievement.

7. **Service and personal well-being connection:** Research from the University of Michigan demonstrates that individuals who engage in regular helping behavior show reduced mortality risk and improved mental health outcomes. Studies indicate that the helper's high phenomenon produces measurable physiological benefits including reduced inflammation and improved immune function.

8. **Routine maintenance during low motivation:** Research from Duke University demonstrates that individuals who maintain beneficial routines regardless of motivation show 67% higher rates of long-term goal achievement. Studies indicate that understanding motivation as unreliable rather than necessary enables more consistent behavior change.

9. **Meta-cognitive hope:** Studies from the University of Pennsylvania show that individuals who maintain hope about their ability to regain hope during difficult periods demonstrate superior long-term resilience. This "hope about hope" creates a psychological safety net that prevents complete despair during temporary setbacks.

10. **Gradual skill integration:** Research in motor learning and skill acquisition shows that expertise develops through small, consistent practice rather than dramatic breakthroughs. Studies demonstrate that individuals who expect gradual progress maintain motivation longer and achieve higher skill levels than those expecting rapid transformation.

10: Hope Lives in Us
Restore, Rebuild, Recommit

The hardest part about rebuilding hope isn't the initial work of establishing new patterns and perspectives. The hardest part is what happens when everything you've built starts to feel fragile again. When the energy you've carefully protected begins to drain. When the habits you've established start to slip. When the opportunities you've seized lead to new challenges that feel overwhelming.

Just like the Greek Temple, sometimes you might need a quick restore, and other times you might be in for a more extensive rehabilitation. This isn't a sign that you've failed or that the WE HOPE framework doesn't work. This is simply how hope operates in real life. Hope isn't a destination you reach and then maintain effortlessly. Hope is a renewable resource that requires regular attention and occasional restoration.[1]

The cyclical nature of hope can feel discouraging when you're experiencing it for the first time after rebuilding. You might think you should be "past" the struggles that brought you to this framework initially. You might feel frustrated that you need to revisit concepts and practices you thought you had mastered. This frustration is understandable, but it's also based on an unrealistic expectation about how personal growth actually works.

One journey that is of particular impact for me is the story of Rebecca. After years of struggling through addiction that almost destroyed her family, Rebecca found hope. With her understanding of hope, and a lot of work in treatment programs, Rebecca ended a 20-year stint of addiction, and she just recently celebrated her tenth year of sobriety. Is her life perfect? Far from it, but she has hope to keep applying what she now understands and knows as truth and to keep fighting for a life that she knows she deserves.

Rebecca has also become a beacon for others. She has helped hundreds of people navigate their own addictions, patiently guiding them back to hope where they can rebuild the skills necessary for a life beyond drugs. Her story illustrates a crucial truth that hope doesn't just heal us, but it transforms us into healers for others.[2]

Understanding that hope fades and returns in waves helps you prepare for your own inevitable seasons of difficulty. Instead of being caught off guard when hope feels distant again, you can recognize the pattern and respond with tools and strategies rather than panic or despair. More importantly, this understanding positions you to become the hope that others in this world so desperately need just to make it through their next day.

Hope Is Cyclical — Expect It

Human psychology and physiology both operate in cycles.[3] Your sleep follows daily cycles. Your energy fluctuates in predictable patterns throughout the day and across seasons. Your motivation waxes and wanes based on countless internal and external factors that you can't fully control.

Hope follows similar patterns because it's connected to all these other cycles. When you're physically depleted, emotionally drained, or mentally overwhelmed, your hope naturally becomes less accessible. When you're dealing with major life transitions, unexpected challenges, or even positive changes that require significant adaptation, your hope resources get stretched thin.

However, the cyclical nature of hope doesn't mean you're back to square one when it fades. Each time you work through the WE HOPE framework, you develop greater skill and efficiency in applying its principles. Each time you rebuild hope, you do so from a higher baseline than before. The cycles become less dramatic and shorter in duration as you gain experience managing them.

Expecting hope to fade periodically actually strengthens your overall resilience.[4] When you know that difficult seasons are temporary and that you have tools to navigate them, you don't waste energy fighting the reality of your current state. Instead, you can focus that energy on the specific actions that will help you move through the cycle more quickly.

This cyclical understanding also helps you appreciate the seasons when hope feels strong and accessible. You don't take these periods for granted because you understand they require maintenance and won't last indefinitely without attention. This awareness helps you make better use of high-hope seasons to prepare for the times when hope feels more elusive.

The cycles of hope often correspond to larger life transitions. Major changes in relationships, career, health, or living situations can trigger periods when hope needs rebuilding. Understanding this connection helps you normalize the experience and respond proactively rather than reactively.

Some cycles are predictable based on your personal patterns and triggers. You might notice that hope tends to fade during certain seasons of the year, anniversary dates of difficult experiences, or periods of high stress at work. Identifying these patterns allows you to prepare with additional support and intentional practices.

Other cycles are triggered by unexpected events you couldn't have predicted or prevented. Loss, illness, job changes, relationship difficulties, or global crises can all impact your hope levels regardless of how well you've been maintaining your foundation. These unpredictable cycles require flexibility and self-compassion as you adapt your approach to meet new circumstances.

The key to managing cyclical hope lies in developing what psychologists call "psychological flexibility"—the ability to adapt your responses based on current circumstances rather than rigidly applying the same strategies regardless of context.[5] Sometimes you need to focus more intensively on protecting your energy. Sometimes you need to rebuild habits that have fallen away. Sometimes you need to actively seek new opportunities or perspectives.

Understanding hope's cyclical nature also transforms how you support others who are struggling. When someone you care about is going through a difficult period, you can offer perspective about the temporary nature of their current state without minimizing their experience. You can share your own experiences with hope cycles without making it about you. You can provide practical support that acknowledges both their current needs and their underlying strength.

You Are Hope

This new understanding brings us to the most profound realization of your journey. The next cycle of hope in your life is to understand that you are not merely someone who has found hope. You have become hope itself, walking in the world.

The journey through this book has taken you from the depths of hopelessness to the heights of possibility. You've learned that hope isn't a feeling that happens to you but a skill you can develop. You've discovered that worth isn't earned but inherent, that energy can be protected and renewed, that small habits create lasting change, that opportunities exist even in difficult circumstances, that perspective shapes reality, and that serving others completes your own healing.

This realization might feel overwhelming or even unbelievable. After all, you likely picked up this book because hope felt distant or lost. You may have felt broken, exhausted, or disconnected from your purpose. The idea that you could be a source of hope for others might seem impossible when you're still working on rebuilding hope in your own life.

However, that's exactly why you are qualified to be hope for others. Your struggles don't disqualify you from being a source of light in the world. They prepare you for it. The darkness you've walked through gives you credibility when you extend a hand to someone else who's lost their way. The healing you've done makes you a living example that change is possible. The hope you've rebuilt becomes a beacon for others who are still searching.

The Power of Integrity

To understand how you become hope for others, we need to examine the foundation that makes this possible. That foundation is integrity, and it's built through the promises you make and keep to yourself.

The Latin root of integrity means to be complete or whole. What a lovely. beautiful concept! When you live your life with integrity, you are whole and complete. The word has the same roots as integrate, integer, and integral. You connect with your purpose, your values, and all the Pillars of Hope. This wholeness isn't about perfection or having all your problems solved. It's about alignment between your values, your commitments, and your actions. When these three elements work together, you experience the deep satisfaction that comes from living authentically.

Most people think of integrity as simply being honest with others, and while that's certainly part of it, the integrity that rebuilds hope starts with honesty with yourself. It's the willingness to see your situation clearly, acknowledge your struggles without shame, and commit to doing something about them even when you don't feel ready.

Throughout this book, you've been practicing integrity each time you chose to keep reading instead of giving up. Each time you completed a reflection exercise instead of skipping it. Each time you tried a new approach instead of falling back into old patterns. These small acts of keeping promises to yourself have been building your capacity for integrity.

Integrity develops through repetition and consistency.[6] Every time you follow through on a commitment you've made to yourself, you strengthen your self-trust. Every time you act in alignment with your values, even when it's difficult, you reinforce your sense of wholeness. Every time you choose growth over comfort, you demonstrate to yourself that you are someone who can be relied upon.

This self-trust becomes the foundation for everything else. When you know you can count on yourself to follow through, you're willing to set bigger goals and take greater risks. When you trust your own judgment, you're less dependent on external validation. When you believe in your ability to handle whatever comes, you can offer that stability to others.

The beautiful paradox of integrity is that it simultaneously makes you both more independent and more connected. As you become more aligned with yourself, you become more capable of authentic relationships. As you learn to trust yourself, others learn to trust you as well. As you become complete within yourself, you have more to offer the world around you.

Living with integrity doesn't absolve you of ever making mistakes or ensure that you always handle everything perfectly. It means you take responsibility for your choices, learn from your errors, and keep working toward alignment. It means you show up consistently, even when you don't feel like it. It means you honor your commitments to yourself and others, even when it requires sacrifice.

The person who lives with integrity becomes a source of hope simply by existing. In a world where so many people are disconnected from their values, struggling with follow-through, and living reactive lives, someone who demonstrates consistent alignment becomes an inspiration to others. You don't have to preach or teach or try to fix anyone. Your life itself becomes a testament to what's possible.

This is how you become hope for others. We don't become hope through grand gestures or perfect living, but through the persistence of showing up authentically, doing what you say you'll do, and continuing to grow even when it's hard. Your integrity gives others permission to expect more from themselves. Your wholeness reminds others that they too can find alignment.

The challenge I want to leave you with is simple but not easy: commit to living a life of complete integrity. Begin with small promises to yourself and keep them religiously. Align your daily choices with your deepest values. Take responsibility for your growth and healing without waiting for perfect conditions. Embrace and put into practice the Pillars of Hope. Last, show up as the person you're becoming, not just the person you've been. I know life is tough and challenging, but we need people of integrity if we are to have any sort of hope in this world. We need integrity for ourselves, for our families, and for our communities.

This challenge shouldn't feel like being more than yourself, seeking attention, or boasting about your accomplishments. It should feel like you're becoming integrated into your community. It's about closing the gap between who you are and who you're capable of being. It's about living so authentically that your very presence reminds others of their own potential.

What We All Hope For

After years of working with people who have lost their hope and found it again, I've discovered something remarkable. Despite our different backgrounds, circumstances, and struggles, we all hope for fundamentally the same things. These universal longings connect us across every barrier and remind us of our shared humanity.[7]

For years, I wondered what I would do with my life if I chose a path outside of the education system. I could never figure it out because teaching isn't what I do. It's who I am. It's what I always wanted to be. I continue to teach, and I hope to be able to live my purpose through teaching for a lot longer. I find it fulfilling and rewarding, and I don't want to lose that. Yet, I also desire to keep teaching the world about hope, even if my message only reaches a room full of high school kids on an annual basis. It's who I am, and it keeps me going.

Research in positive psychology has identified the core elements that create meaning and satisfaction in human life. These findings align perfectly with what I've observed in my own work and what I've seen in the lives of people who successfully rebuild hope. We all hope for connection, inspiration, love, and the opportunity to make a difference.

Connection might be the most fundamental human need.[8] We hope for relationships where we can be truly known and accepted. We long for communities where we belong. We want to feel understood and to understand others. When hope fades, it's often because connection has been severed. When hope returns, it's usually because connection has been restored.

This connection isn't just about having people around you. It's about feeling genuinely seen and valued for who you are. It's about being able to share your struggles without judgment and your successes without envy. It's about knowing that your presence matters to someone and that their presence matters to you.

Inspiration is another universal longing. We hope to be moved by beauty, challenged by growth, and motivated by possibility. We want to feel that life has meaning beyond survival and comfort. We long to be part of something larger than ourselves. We hope to both give and receive encouragement that helps us continue when things get difficult.

Love, in all its forms, represents perhaps our deepest hope. We hope to love and be loved. We hope to care for others and to be cared for in return. We hope to experience the vulnerability and trust that deep relationships require. We hope to know that we matter enough to someone that they would choose us again and again.

Making a difference gives our lives purpose and direction. We hope that our existence improves the world in some way. We want to know that our struggles weren't meaningless and that our growth can benefit others. We hope to leave things better than we found them, whether that's in our families, our communities, or our chosen fields of work.

These hopes aren't naive or unrealistic. They're the natural expressions of healthy human development. When people lose hope, it's often because they've started to believe these longings are impossible or that they don't deserve to experience them. The work of rebuilding hope is largely the work of reconnecting with these fundamental desires, applying the WE HOPE Pillars, and creating pathways to fulfill them.

The beautiful truth is that these hopes are interconnected. When you experience genuine connection, you're more likely to feel inspired. When you feel inspired, you're more capable of giving and receiving love. When you experience love, you're more motivated to make a difference. When you make a difference, you create more opportunities for connection. The cycle reinforces itself.

What's remarkable is how achievable these hopes become when you approach them through the WE HOPE framework. As you recognize your worth, you become capable of deeper connection. As you protect your energy, you have more to offer in relationships. As you build sustaining habits, you create stability that allows love to flourish. As you seize opportunities, you find ways to make a meaningful difference. As you shift your perspective, you recognize inspiration all around you. As you serve others, you experience all of these hopes simultaneously.

Your journey through this book has been preparing you to experience these universal longings more fully. More importantly, it's been preparing you to help others access them as well. When you live with connection, inspiration, love, and purpose, you become a demonstration of what's possible. You become hope walking in the world.

Now Is Just Beginning

If you're reading these words, you might be able to see a path out of the darkness. You may not be completely healed, you may still have challenges to face, but you're no longer the person who first opened this book. You've grown, you've learned, you've changed. You've proven to yourself that transformation is possible.

This ending is actually a beginning. Everything you've learned, every skill you've developed, every insight you've gained becomes the foundation for the next chapter of your life. The hope you've rebuilt isn't a destination you've reached but a capacity you'll continue to strengthen.

Your story matters more than you know. The struggles you've faced and overcome become a source of credibility when you help others. The healing you've experienced becomes evidence that healing is possible. The hope you've rebuilt becomes a light that others can follow when they're lost in their own darkness.

You might not see yourself as someone who helps others find hope. You might think that role belongs to therapists, counselors, coaches, or other helping professionals, but the truth is that the most powerful sources of hope are often people who have walked similar paths and found their way through.

Your coworker who notices you handling stress differently than you used to might ask what's changed. Your friend who sees you pursuing new opportunities might wonder how you found the courage. Your family member who observes your increased energy and purpose might want to know your secret. These conversations become opportunities to share hope.

You don't need special training or credentials to be a source of hope for others. You need authenticity, vulnerability, and the willingness to share what you've learned. You need to remember what it felt like when hope was missing from your life and be willing to sit with others in their darkness while pointing toward the light.

I have always felt that I am average personified. I am just your typical, everyday, run-of-the-mill high school teacher. What did I have to share that is inspiring or life-changing? We tend to think that inspiring acts can only be done by those who have overcome the toughest of challenges, whose deeds warrant making headlines. It's time to stop the hero worship. We should all be inspired more by the ordinary acts of our loved ones than by the manufactured reels of our celebrities. We all can and should be an inspiration because we act out of hope on a daily basis.[9]

In my own work, I've spent the last 20 years helping students and adults reach their full potential. I have received awards for my dedication as a public school teacher. I have earned promotions professionally. In my personal life, I am part of a loving, healthy relationship with my wife, and I am fortunate to have some of the best kids. My children are wise and thoughtful about how they interact with the world. They make good choices and are good examples to others.

From the outside, my life might seem perfect, and if I'm being honest, I am fortunate enough to say that my life really is very fulfilling. Like any family, we have our ups and downs. My daughter is navigating those challenging teenage years. We are constantly faced with tough financial decisions. We compare our lives to other people's too frequently. However, I wouldn't trade those challenges away for anything.

I don't share this to place myself on a pedestal or to minimize others who are struggling. I share it because WE HOPE and its pillars will work for the betterment of your life. I don't live the life of high-profile influencer or a celebrity guru. My message is that anyone living with hope can be a hero to somebody.

You may not feel like a hero. You may not even feel finished, but the ripple effects of your healing extend far beyond what you can see. Your children, if you have them, will benefit from your increased emotional stability and purpose. Your friends will experience you as more present and supportive. Your community will be enriched by your contributions. People you haven't even met yet will be affected by the hope you carry.

This is how hope spreads in the world. Not through massive movements or dramatic interventions, but through individuals who have done their own work and are willing to help others do theirs. We find hope through people who have found their way out of despair and are willing to serve as guides for others who are still lost.

Your story of losing hope and finding it again becomes a resource for the world. Every time you share it appropriately, you plant seeds of possibility in someone else's life. Every time you demonstrate what's possible through your own living, you give others permission to believe in their own potential.

The person you're becoming has responsibilities you may not have considered. You have a responsibility to continue growing, not just for yourself but for everyone whose life you'll touch. You have a responsibility to stay connected to your purpose, not just for your own fulfillment but as an example of what purposeful living looks like. You have a responsibility to maintain your hope, not just for your own well-being but as a resource for others who will need it.

These responsibilities aren't burdens but privileges. You get to be part of the solution to the hopelessness that plagues our world. You get to contribute to the healing that our communities desperately need. You get to be living proof that change is possible, that healing happens, and that hope can be rebuilt.

In the end, we hope for you. We hope that you'll continue growing, continue healing, and continue becoming the person you're meant to be. We hope that you'll remember your worth when the world tries to convince you otherwise. We hope that you'll prioritize your energy and use it wisely. We hope that you'll maintain the habits that serve your growth. We hope that you'll seize the opportunities that align with your purpose. We hope that you'll keep the perspective that serves your highest good. We hope that you'll continue serving others as a way of completing your own healing.

Most of all, we hope that you'll remember who you are. You are not someone who needs to be fixed. You are someone who has already begun the work of transformation. Stone by stone, you are someone who is courageously rebuilding. You are not someone who has nothing to offer. You are someone whose very existence makes the world more hopeful. You are becoming a pillar to your community.

You're just beginning. Just like the ancient Greeks and their glorious buildings, the temple of your life is waiting for you to build it. Construct each pillar with purpose, connection, growth, and service. Fill each day with the hope you've worked so hard to rebuild. Remember that when you live authentically, facing every challenge with courage, recognizing every person you help along the way, you are building the Pillars of Hope that the world desperately needs.

You are the hope that WE HOPE for!

Stone Upon Stone—Building Your Pillar

Base

Hope Sustainability Assessment:

Complete this research-based assessment to understand how your current perspective may be supporting or hindering your hope. For each statement, rate yourself on a scale of 1-5 (1 = never true, 5 = always

1. I recognize when my hope is beginning to fade and respond with tools rather than panic
2. I can maintain perspective during difficult seasons, remembering they are temporary
3. I keep promises I make to myself, even small ones
4. My actions consistently align with my stated values and commitments
5. I can offer support to others without depleting my own resources
6. I believe my struggles have equipped me to help others facing similar challenges
7. I can share my story appropriately when it might benefit someone else
8. I maintain hope-supporting routines even during high-stress periods
9. I see myself as someone who has valuable experiences and insights to offer
10. I understand that being hope for others is a responsibility and a privilege

Reflection Questions:

After completing the assessment, reflect on these questions:

°   Which statements scored lowest for you? What patterns do you notice about your hope sustainability?
°   Think about Rebecca's story from the chapter. What parallels do you see between her journey and yours?
°   Complete this sentence honestly: "I would feel more prepared to be hope for others if I could stop believing that_____."
°   Recall a time when someone served as hope for you during a dark period. What did they do that made the difference?

Integrity Inventory:

Examine the foundation that makes sustainable hope possible by reflecting on these areas:

- **Promises to Yourself:** What small commitments have you made and kept recently? What promises have you broken?
- **Values Alignment:** Where do your daily actions most closely match your deepest values? Where is there a gap?
- **Authentic Living:** When do you feel most like yourself versus when do you feel like you're performing?
- **Growth Mindset:** How do you typically respond when you make mistakes or face setbacks?

Write 2-3 sentences about your current relationship with integrity in each area.

Column

The Becoming Hope Challenge:
This challenge will help you develop the capacity to maintain hope through cycles and begin serving as hope for others.

Days 1-3: Integrity Foundation Building

Each day, focus on one small promise to yourself that builds your integrity foundation:

- Day 1: Choose one tiny habit that aligns with your values (5-minute morning reflection, glass of water upon waking, etc.) and follow through
- Day 2: When you make a mistake, practice self-compassion instead of self-criticism
- Day 3: Identify one area where your actions don't match your values and take one small corrective step

For each day, document:

- What promise did you keep to yourself?
- How did it feel to follow through despite not feeling motivated?
- What resistance or excuses came up, and how did you work with them?

Days 4-6: Hope Cycle Recognition

Practice recognizing and responding to natural hope fluctuations:

- Day 4: Notice your energy and hope levels throughout the day. When do they naturally ebb and flow?
- Day 5: When you catch yourself in negative spiraling, consciously apply one pillar from the WE HOPE framework

- Day 6: Prepare for tomorrow's challenges by choosing which pillar(s) you'll emphasize

Daily Reflection Questions:
- How did my hope levels change throughout the day, and what influenced these changes?
- Which pillar felt most supportive during low moments?
- What evidence did I create that I can navigate hope cycles with tools rather than despair?

Days 7-10: Serving as Hope
Practice being hope for others in small, sustainable ways:
- Day 7: Share encouragement with someone who's struggling (without trying to fix their problems)
- Day 8: Tell someone about a lesson you learned from a difficult experience (when appropriate)
- Day 9: Demonstrate one of the WE HOPE pillars through your actions where others can observe
- Day 10: Create a simple plan for how you'll continue being hope for others moving forward

For each interaction, note:
- How did you feel before, during, and after serving as hope for someone else?
- What resistance came up about sharing your journey or offering support?
- How did the other person respond to your authenticity?
- What did you learn about your capacity to help others?

Daily Integration Practice: Each evening, spend 5 minutes answering:
- How did I honor both my own hope needs and my responsibility to others today?
- What evidence did I create that I'm becoming someone others can count on?
- Which of the four universal longings (connection, inspiration, love, making a difference) did I experience or facilitate today?
- How is my understanding of what it means to be hope evolving?

End-of-Challenge Integration: After 10 days, reflect on:
- How has your relationship with the cyclical nature of hope changed?

- ° What evidence do you have that integrity strengthens your foundation?
- ° In what ways do you feel prepared to serve as hope for others?
- ° What sustainable practices will you continue to maintain your role as someone who carries hope?
- ° How might your story of rebuilding hope serve the world around you?

Capstone

Books:

Let Your Life Speak by Parker Palmer

The Lightmaker's Manifesto by Karen Walrond

Make Your Life a Story Worth Telling by Mark Batterson

Braiding Sweetgrass by Robin Wall Kimmerer

Podcasts:

How to Be a Better Human

On Purpose with Jay Shetty

Living Fully with Mallory Ervin

Sounds True: Insights at the Edge

Articles:

"How Legacy Shapes Our Lives" (Greater Good Magazine)

"The Role of Hope in Moral Imagination" (Stanford Ethics Lab)

"Purpose-Driven Living" (New York Times Opinion)

"Narrative Identity and Hope" (Journal of Humanistic Psychology)

Chapter Notes:

1. **Hope as renewable resource:** Research in positive psychology demonstrates that hope operates as a dynamic capacity rather than a fixed state. Studies from the University of Kansas show that hope can be depleted through overuse or neglect but can also be restored through intentional practices, similar to physical fitness or cognitive abilities.

2. **Post-traumatic growth and helping others:** Research from the University of North Carolina demonstrates that individuals who experience significant personal transformation often develop what researchers call "helper therapy principle"—where helping others heal becomes part of their own continued recovery. Studies show that individuals in recovery who help others maintain higher rates of long-term success.

3. **Cyclical patterns in human psychology:** Research in chronobiology demonstrates that human psychological and physiological processes operate in predictable cycles, including circadian rhythms, seasonal patterns, and longer developmental cycles. Studies show that understanding these natural fluctuations helps individuals better prepare for and manage periods of difficulty.

4. **Resilience and expectation setting:** Research from the University of Pennsylvania shows that individuals who maintain realistic expectations about the cyclical nature of challenges demonstrate significantly higher psychological resilience. Studies indicate that expecting periodic difficulties reduces the psychological impact of setbacks and speeds recovery time.

5. **Psychological flexibility:** Research from the Association for Contextual Behavioral Science demonstrates that psychological flexibility—the ability to adapt responses based on current circumstances—is one of the strongest predictors of mental health and life satisfaction. Studies show that flexible thinking patterns prevent rigid responses that can worsen difficult situations.

6. **Self-trust and behavioral consistency:** Research from Stanford University demonstrates that individuals who consistently follow through on small commitments to themselves develop measurably higher self-efficacy and confidence. Studies show that this self-trust creates a foundation for larger goal achievement and better relationships with others.

7. **Universal human needs:** Research in self-determination theory identifies three basic psychological needs shared across all cultures: autonomy, competence, and relatedness. Multiple cross-cultural studies confirm that fulfillment of these universal needs predicts well-being regardless of cultural background or personal circumstances.

8. **Connection as fundamental need:** The Harvard Study of Adult Development, spanning over 80 years, demonstrates that social connection is the primary predictor of happiness and life satisfaction over time. Research shows that individuals with strong relationships live longer, experience better physical health, and maintain cognitive function better than those who are socially isolated.

9. **Ordinary heroism research:** Studies from the American Psychological Association demonstrate that everyday acts of kindness and consistency have measurable positive impacts on both givers and receivers. Research shows that "everyday heroes" who consistently help others in small ways create significant community-level improvements in mental health and social cohesion.

Find more **resources,**
opportunities to **collaborate with
Dustin Drake,**
additional **WE HOPE Guidebooks**
and more
at
whatWEHOPEfor.com

www.ingramcontent.com/pod-product-compliance
Lightning Source LLC
Chambersburg PA
CBHW051514120626
46551CB00012B/915